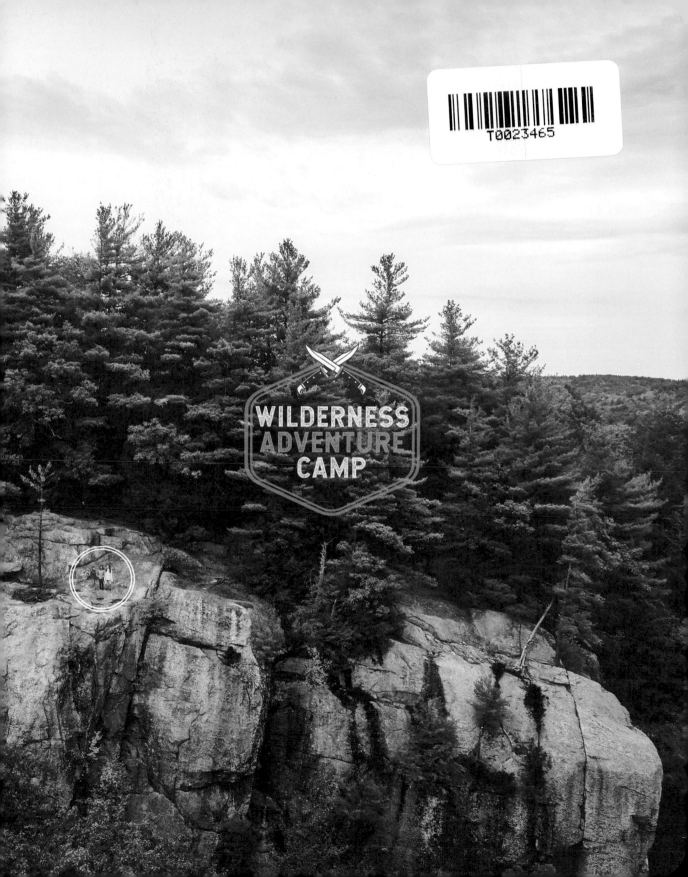

WILDERNESS ADVENTURE CAMP

ESSENTIAL OUTDOOR SURVIVAL SKILLS FOR KIDS

FRANK GRINDROD

PHOTOGRAPHS BY JARED LEEDS

Storey Publishing

The mission of Storey Publishing is to serve our customers by publishing practical information that encourages personal independence in harmony with the environment.

Edited by Deanna F. Cook, Lisa H. Hiley, Michal Lumsden, and Corey Cusson
Art direction and book design by Carolyn Eckert
Text production by Liseann Karandisecky
Indexed by Christine R. Lindemer, Boston Road Communications

Cover and interior photography by © Jared Leeds Photography
Additional photography credits appear on page 159
Prop management by Liseann Karandisecky
Illustrations by © Steve Sanford, with additional illustrations by Ilona Sherratt
© Storey Publishing, 46–47, 72–83, 98, 128, 129

Text © 2021 by Frank Grindrod

Storey Publishing
210 MASS MoCA Way
North Adams, MA 01247
storey.com

Printed in China by R.R. Donnelley
10 9 8 7 6 5 4 3 2

Library of Congress Cataloging-in-Publication Data
   on file

Storey books are available at special discounts when purchased in bulk for premiums and sales promotions as well as for fund-raising or educational use. Special editions or book excerpts can also be created to specification. For details, please call 800-827-8673, or send an email to sales@storey.com.

I'm excited that you have picked up this book!

I give tremendous gratitude to all the present and former staff of Earthwork Programs who helped improve the culture and programing over these last 20 years and to all the students and families who have supported this vision and trusted us with their children. We cherish our relationships with kids who started in elementary school and who, year after year, continue to give themselves to this important work. My love to you all.

CONTENTS

Welcome to Wilderness Survival 9

CHAPTER 1:
GET READY FOR ADVENTURE 11

CHAPTER 2:
MUST-HAVE SKILLS 29

FINDING YOUR WAY 30

USING A KNIFE 38

BUILDING A FIRE 56

TYING KNOTS 70

CHAPTER 3:
SETTING UP CAMP 85

CHAPTER 4:
CAMP CRAFT 117

CHAPTER 5:
FOOD & DRINK 137

debris hut

WELCOME TO WILDERNESS SURVIVAL

I'm excited that we will be going on a wilderness adventure together. You might have been on a camping trip before, but it was probably your parents or some other adult who made the plans for your adventure. Well, now it's your turn!

No matter how far you're going or how long you'll be gone — even if you'll just be camping in your own backyard overnight — there are certain things you'll need to bring with you and other things you'll need to learn.

Here are the essentials for your trip:

- The right mind-set for adventure and survival

- Your survival kit

- Skills to be comfortable and confident

How do you find out where to get these things? From a guide, of course! It's important to learn from someone who has traveled the path before you. For many years, I've been teaching kids to survive in the woods, and I'll teach you the most important tips and lessons in this book! Look for my tried-and-true Tips from the Guide throughout the book for extra information.

On any journey, there will be challenges that may be outside your comfort zone. For example, in the book *My Side of the Mountain,* Sam left the city to live in the Catskill Mountains. He built a shelter, made fires, learned what to eat, and figured out how to take care of his needs — all things he had never done before. Even though he struggled sometimes, he made it through his amazing adventure!

This book is your call to **ADVENTURE**. Are you ready? Let's begin!

1

GET READY FOR ADVENTURE

You can have an adventure just about anywhere, from your own backyard to a state park to deep wilderness. Wherever you're camping, it's important to be prepared with the right clothing and gear.

CLOTHING

Proper clothing is a very important part of your equipment when you're out in the woods. There is an old saying that goes, "There is no such thing as bad weather, only bad clothing." Whether the weather is hot and sunny, rainy and windy, or cold and snowy, the right clothing and accessories will keep you safe and comfortable.

The most important thing to remember is to try to avoid cotton. Cotton, which is what most T-shirts and jeans are made of, is usually comfortable, but when it gets wet (even from you sweating as you hike or make camp), it gets cold and heavy and takes a long time to dry. If the weather is nice and you're not going too far from home, it's fine to wear cotton clothing. But if it's rainy or snowy, or you're going on a long hike or a camping trip, there are lots of better choices for what to wear. Check clothing labels for materials like silk, wool, polyester, nylon, wool, acrylic — they are better at keeping you warm and dry.

TIP FROM THE GUIDE
LAYER UP AND DOWN

When you're moving around a lot, your body temperature goes up, even if it's cold outside. Sweating can be dangerous in cold weather because the dampness will soak into your clothes and make you chilled when you stop to rest. When you're outside moving around and you feel yourself heating up, remove a layer or two so you don't get too hot and sweaty. Put the layers back on when you start to feel cold again or when you stop to rest. Adjust layers to suit the weather and your level of comfort.

LAYER, LAYER, LAYER

Lots of people underestimate how cold they can get when they're out in the wilderness. Even if it seems like a mild day outside, a little bit of rain, wind, or snow can make you cold very quickly. The secret to staying warm and dry in the wilderness is to dress in layers. Here are the three key layers:

The base layer is next to your skin (think long underwear in the winter). It should be made of thin, lightweight material like silk, polypropylene, and/or lightweight wool. These materials *wick* (pull) moisture away from your skin to evaporate, which helps regulate your body temperature.

The insulation layer is meant to create a layer of air that will trap body heat. It should be puffy or heavier than your base layer and fit well but not too tightly. It's important to have a little bit of air under the insulation layer that can heat up with you. Tight clothing that restricts your movement can make it harder for you to stay warm. Choose a shirt made of fleece or wool, or a jacket or vest with a down or synthetic filler.

The outer layer, or shell, shields you from wind and rain. Some waterproof materials, like rubber or coated nylon, trap lots of body heat and might make you sweaty when you're active. Others, like Gore-Tex, can "breathe," which means a fabric lets moisture out while keeping heat in. Jackets that advertise "breathability" are much better at letting sweat evaporate off your body, making you much more comfortable. Any jacket that is waterproof is also windproof and will protect you from windchill. For winter hiking and camping, an outer layer for your legs is a good idea.

base
layer

insulation
layer

outer
layer

HEAD AND HANDS

Protecting your head and hands is just as important as the rest of your body.

Hats are a critical part of your gear, whatever the season. You might have heard that we lose most of our body heat through our heads. That's not exactly true, but leaving your head (and neck) uncovered in cold weather will definitely make you feel colder. A good warm hat will be made of wool, fleece, polyester, or other materials besides cotton. Just remember you can take your hat off if your head is getting too sweaty.

In the summer, a lightweight hat or baseball cap shades your eyes and face from the sun. You can dip it in water for added coolness or put insect repellent on the brim.

Sunglasses are good to have if you are out in strong sun, even in winter. The glare of sunlight reflecting off of bright, white snow makes it hard to see and can hurt your eyes. It can even give you a sunburn, so you might want to put some sunscreen on your nose and cheeks, too!

Gloves and mittens are made with lots of different materials and features, so it's helpful to remember the basic pros and cons of each: With gloves, your fingers are separated, so you can use your hands better to work on things but your fingers will get colder over time. With mittens, since your fingers are all together in one space, your hands and fingers will stay warmer, but it's harder to do delicate work with mittens on!

DON'T FORGET YOUR FEET

For most hiking and camping, you can't go wrong with low-cut hiking shoes. If the weather is really nice and warm, you can also wear trail-running shoes with flexible soles. Some hiking boots have higher ankles, which is a trade-off: Higher ankles might protect you from rolling or spraining an ankle, but they can make it harder to run and jump. With lower-cut shoes, your ankles will become stronger the more you wear them.

On a long hike or camping trip, it's helpful to bring a pair of comfortable waterproof boots or strap-on sandals or "water shoes" with you. That way, if you have to hike through a swamp or cross a brook or river, you can take off your hiking shoes (and socks) and wear the rubber boots or water shoes just to get through the water. Then, you can take a break to dry off your feet before putting your socks and hiking shoes back on. And sandals can double as camp shoes.

Hats also keep bugs out of your hair.

GOOD SOCKS

Always wear durable hiking socks that fit properly. Good socks will help prevent blisters and help keep your feet nice and dry. Most good hiking socks are made of wool and/or nylon. They can be thick, lightweight, or even "ultralight" and very thin. The colder it is outside, the thicker your socks should be.

If you're going on a long hike in the wintertime or when it's really cold outside, you can even wear very thin "liner socks" underneath a pair of thick wool socks.

No matter the weather or temperature outside, make sure your foot feels nice and snug in your hiking boot or shoe, without being too tight. If your boots are too loose and your foot slides around too much, you'll start to get blisters.

TIP FROM THE GUIDE

THESE BOOTS WERE MADE FOR . . . SQUATTING?

Before you buy a pair of hiking boots, make sure they fit properly. Squat down in them a few times. See how it feels to kneel down and put a knee on the ground, and to get up and down from the ground. Walk around the store — some places have an area where you can test the boots by walking on an incline. Don't buy boots that pinch anywhere or dig into your heel. If they aren't comfortable in the store, they're unlikely to get more comfortable while you're hiking.

compass

whistle

head-lamp

strike-anywhere matches

paracord

lighter

water bottle

signal mirror

bandana

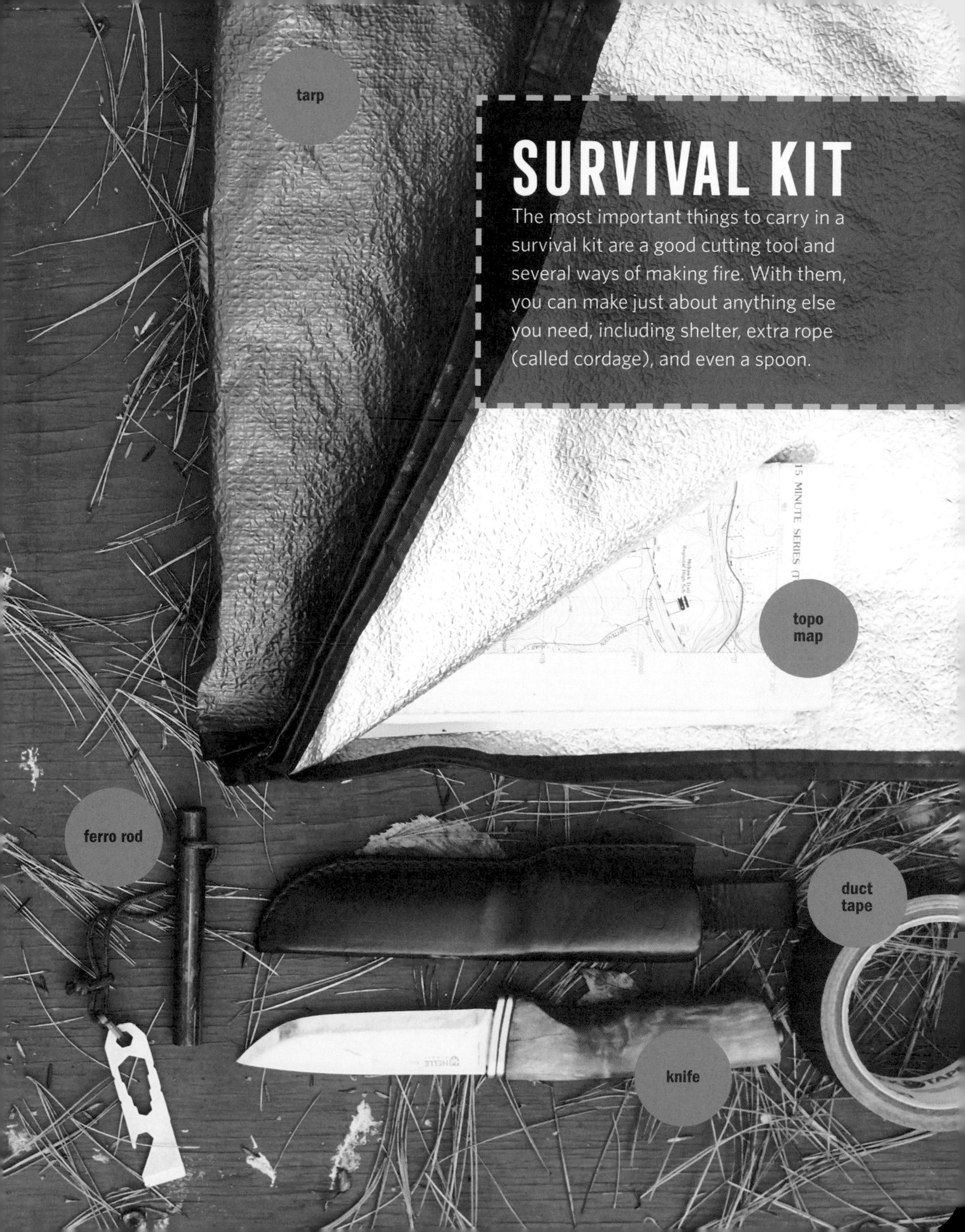

tarp

SURVIVAL KIT

The most important things to carry in a survival kit are a good cutting tool and several ways of making fire. With them, you can make just about anything else you need, including shelter, extra rope (called cordage), and even a spoon.

topo map

ferro rod

duct tape

knife

point

tip

spine

edge

bevel

heel

handle

tang

The tang is the part of the blade that extends into the handle of the knife.

A blade with a Scandi grind edge, as shown here, has a distinctive bevel that is easy for even beginners to sharpen.

A G😊D KNIFE

With a proper cutting tool, you can do just about everything you need to do to survive. It's important to complete the knife safety contract on page 39 before you use any kind of knife.

You can use a folding pocketknife with a locking blade, such as a Swiss Army knife, for many of the skills you'll learn in this book. For some activities, though, you will need a sturdy knife with a fully extended blade that you store in a sheath (a protective case) when you're not using it. Your knife should have a three-quarter or full "tang," which is the metal part of the blade that goes into the handle. A full tang means the metal part extends the full length of the handle.

Choose a knife with a stainless or carbon steel blade no longer than about 4 inches (or the size of your palm). A blade with a Scandi grind edge works well for carving and other outdoor uses. That means the blade has a wide bevel (the part that tapers toward the edge) that is easy to sharpen.

WILDERNESS WISDOM
WHAT'S IN A NAME?

In the Tzutuhil Mayan culture of Guatemala's western highlands, a knife is known as "the tooth of the earth." Many Tzutujil people have such reverence for this useful tool that they name their knives.

striking a ferro rod

To learn how to build and start a fire with your kit, go to page 56.

FIRE-MAKING KIT

Making a fire is one of the most valuable skills you can have in the wilderness. Even without shelter, a fire can be very important and helpful, so you should always have the tools and abilities to make one. To make sure you can start a fire even if some of your materials are wet, always carry a couple of different fire-making tools. Bring strike-anywhere matches, packed in a waterproof bag, and a lighter. In addition, a ferro rod (also called a firesteel or metal match) is very useful.

Ferro rods are made of ferrocerium, a man-made metallic alloy that produces sparks of 3,000°F/1,650°C (or hotter) when scraped with something rough or sharp. Ferro rods work without lighter fluid and can start a fire even when wet. A ¾-inch-thick rod gets the best results.

TARP OR OTHER COVERING

grommet

A tarp or cover is a handy piece of waterproof material that can shade you from the sun and protect you from wind, rain, and snow. You can transform it into a backpack, bucket, chair, or an emergency stretcher. A brightly colored one can be a signal in an emergency. A lightweight tarp or drop cloth, a large piece of plastic, or even a big poncho will work.

The best kind of cover is coated nylon with reinforced "grommets," the little metal rings on the corners and along the sides that you can run cord through. Some tarps also have a silver thermal reflective side to help keep in warmth when used close to your body.

Each person should have their own 10 × 10-foot tarp. Use additional ones to create different areas in your camp.

PARACHUTE CORD

This strong, versatile nylon rope is made with seven interwoven strands covered with an outer layer. Commonly called "paracord," it has many uses, such as securing a shelter, lashing together a tripod, hanging equipment, making a fishing net, and more.

arm span

TIP FROM THE GUIDE
HOW MUCH CORD?

When you go out on a wilderness adventure, bring at least seven arm spans of paracord. You can easily cut it to different lengths as you need it.

1. To measure, hold the end of the paracord securely in your right hand. Holding the cord loosely in your left hand, stretch your arms fully apart. This is one arm span.

2. Keeping hold with your left hand, drop the end of the paracord from your right hand. Bring your hands together in front of you.

3. Grip the cord with your right hand and pull more cord through your left hand, as before, until your arms are fully extended.

4. Repeat steps 2 and 3 five more times.

#1 PRINCIPLE: REDUNDANCY

When it comes to your survival kit, *redundancy* means making sure that each piece of gear can be used in many ways. **For example, you can use a bandana . . .**

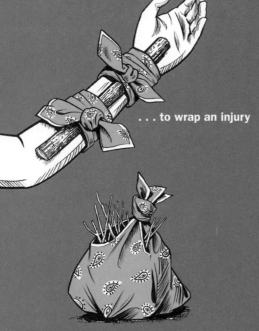

. . . to wrap an injury

. . . as a bag for foraging or collecting tinder

. . . as a pot holder

OTHER EQUIPMENT

Headlamp. This crucial piece of equipment frees up your hands to set up a tarp, cook, or craft in the dark. A flashlight or battery-powered lantern is useful, too. Always pack extra batteries.

Bandana. In addition to keeping the sweat out of your eyes, you can use a bandana to tie things together, carry tinder or edible plants, as a bandage or sling, or in many other ways.

Whistle. Make sure your whistle is durable, loud, and brightly colored so that it's visible if you drop it in leaf litter. Put it on a cord around your neck. (Lots of hiking backpacks have a built-in whistle attached to the chest strap.)

Map and compass. Carry a map and compass even if you have a mapping app on your smartphone or other digital device. Electronics need a power source and a clear satellite signal. You may not have either out in the wilderness. (See page 32 to learn more about using a compass.)

Bathroom kit. Pack a small trowel, a roll of toilet paper, and a container of hand sanitizer. (See page 114 for more details.)

Cooking gear. Camping stores sell a variety of cooking pots and pans. For most meals in the wilderness, a simple pot with a wire handle for hanging it over your fire will do. It can be useful to have one pot to cook food in and one to boil extra water. Many cooking sets have pots that fit together for easier packing and may also come with a pot grabber to use when they're too hot to touch. Some recipes might require a skillet or pie pan, so make sure you have everything you need for the food you brought. Each camper should have a bowl, cup, and eating utensils as well.

Drybag or bear-proof canister. An extra waterproof "drybag" or bear-proof canister is crucial for camping in the wilderness. You can use a drybag to set up a "bear hang" (see page 95) to protect your food from other critters. A bear-proof canister is a secure box or barrel to keep your food in so bears can't break into it. Lots of wilderness areas now require you to use a bear-proof canister (instead of a bear hang) when camping, so always check the local rules and regulations of the area or park you'll be camping in.

Biodegradable soap. A bottle of biodegradable soap can be used for bathing,

cleaning off injuries, and washing dishes. You can even brush your teeth with it! A small container of unscented liquid bleach, tightly sealed and stored in a ziplock bag, allows you to sanitize dishes and can be used in a pinch to purify water.

Water purifying supplies. There are a few different ways of purifying water to make it safe to drink in the wilderness (see page 143). You should always bring at least two different methods of water purification, such as iodine tablets, a UV light, or a filter.

Duct tape. Use it to fix a broken backpack, patch a hole in your tarp or tent, or hold together a bandage. Instead of bringing a big, heavy roll, look for a smaller roll at a camping or hardware store. You can also wrap some duct tape around your water bottle to peel off as you need it.

headlamp

map and compass

bathroom kit

FOOD AND WATER

Obviously, you'll need to bring food and water with you on your camping trip!

Food. Bring foods and meals that are easy to make and easy to eat. Keep in mind that you have to carry out all your trash, so food that comes in cans or lots of packaging will add to your load going home. Packing your supplies in reusable bags saves space and makes it easier to pull out what you need for every meal.

Things like bagels, peanut butter, cheese, granola and trail mix, tortillas, dried (or dehydrated) fruits and vegetables, oatmeal,

Always bring plenty of water with you.

pepperoni or sausage, or jerky are a few ideas for quick, easy snacks and meals while you're out hiking. (See page 144 for some fun snacks to make at your campsite.)

Water. You should always bring at least two 1-liter water bottles with you. Two liters is the amount of water you should be drinking per day when you're getting lots of exercise. Not drinking enough water can make you feel tired, achy, and grumpy and give you headaches. The hotter it is outside, or the more active and sweatier you are, the more water you should be drinking.

(See page 144 for some fun snacks to make at your campsite.)

TIP FROM THE GUIDE
MAKE EVERY CALORIE COUNT

Check the nutrition labels on the foods you buy. Carbohydrates and sugars give you short energy boosts, and fats give you long-term energy. Protein is good for building muscle, but your body will use up more water to digest proteins. If you're out in the cold, you will need lots of extra calories so your body can stay warm.

FIRST-AID KIT

Pack your kit in a brightly colored bag that you can easily find in an emergency. In addition, bring along sunscreen and insect repellent.

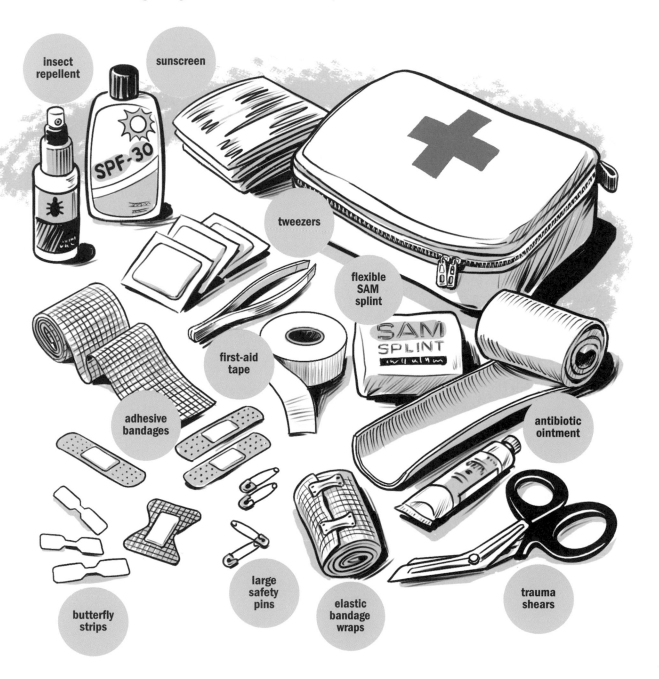

insect repellent

sunscreen

tweezers

flexible SAM splint

first-aid tape

adhesive bandages

antibiotic ointment

butterfly strips

large safety pins

elastic bandage wraps

trauma shears

PACKING YOUR GEAR

The bigger your backpack is, the more stuff you will be tempted to take with you – but carrying lots of extra weight will only slow you down and tire you out. Bring only what you think you'll really need, plus a few extras or backups of certain items in case of emergencies.

Each backpack is different, with different straps, pockets, and compartments, so do what makes the most sense for your gear and your backpack. Here is a general idea of how you might pack efficiently.

TOP OF THE PACK

This part of your backpack is the easiest to access, so pack essentials here that you will want to grab quickly. Make sure you don't overstuff it. A top-heavy pack will throw your balance off.

- **Headlamp & extra batteries**
- **Map & compass**
- **Bandana**
- **Snacks for quick energy**
- **Wallet & phone**
- **Bug spray & sunscreen**
- **First-aid kit**

SIDE POCKETS

These are also easily accessible for small, important items.

- **Water bottles**
- **Water filter**
- **Water shoes or sandals**

BODY OF THE PACK

This is where you'll carry most of your gear. Pack carefully to keep the weight evenly distributed. Putting different kinds of gear and supplies, like clothing and food, in stuff sacks makes it easy to pull out what you need without making a mess of the rest of your belongings.

At the top, put things you might need to get quickly or frequently:

- **Bathroom kit**
- **Jacket, coat, extra gloves & hat, or rain gear**

In the middle, pack heavy items. Put them tightly against the center of your back, to make it easier to hike with the backpack:

- **Food (in a drybag or bear-proof canister)**
- **Cooking gear**

At the bottom, keep the bulkiest items that take up the most space:

- **Clothing**
- **Tarp (or tent, if you are bringing one)**
- **Sleeping bag**
- **Sleeping pad (which you can also strap onto the outside)**

TOP OF THE
PACK
Easy access,
small items

BODY OF THE
PACK
THE TOP
Things you
might need to
get quickly
or frequently

THE MIDDLE
Heavy items

THE BOTTOM
Bulky items

**SIDE
POCKETS**
Water bottle and
other important items

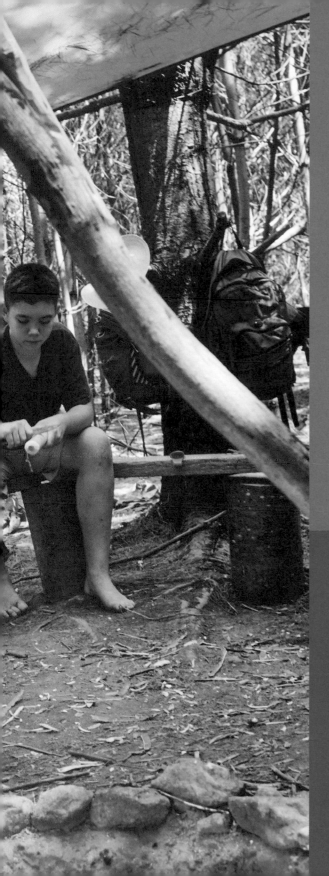

2

MUST-HAVE SKILLS

Mastering the right skills makes the difference between struggling and thriving! Having the right tool for the right job *and* knowing how to use it changes you from a beginner to an expert, someone who can be confident in their abilities. If you can read a compass, safely sharpen and use a knife, successfully build a fire, and tie a few important knots, you will have a solid foundation of skills that you can rely on in any wilderness situation.

FINDING YOUR WAY

When you learn how to use both a map and a compass, you can confidently turn even a small hike into a great exploration.

LOST-PROOFING

A responsible adventurer always thinks ahead and brings the right gear. Two key items for finding your way in the woods are a compass and a topographic map. A topographic (or "topo") map has contour lines that show where the elevation rises and drops. This can help you figure out direction and where you are by land features and scale. Topo maps also show roads, parks, bodies of water, and the names and heights of mountain peaks, all of which you can use to orient yourself.

ANATOMY OF A COMPASS

Baseplate. The flat part that holds the compass.

Scales and rulers. These lines on the baseplate are used to measure distances on a map.

Bezel. The rotating disc that shows north, south, east, and west in a 360-degree circle.

Needle. The magnetic arm that swings to point to the North Magnetic Pole, a shifting iron deposit that currently is about 800 miles south of the geographic North Pole.

Shed. The red symbol where the needle lines up to orient you.

Direction of travel arrow. The arrow on the baseplate that shows you which way to go.

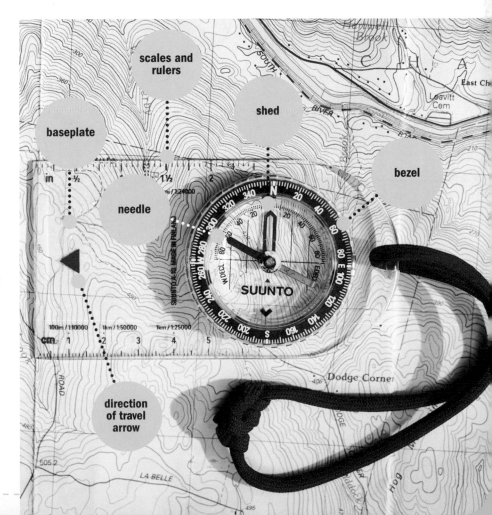

USING YOUR COMPASS

A compass can help you figure out how to get where you want to go when there aren't a lot of signs around to show you the way. Like all outdoor skills, it takes some practice to learn. Here are the basics of what's called "taking a bearing." This allows you to use the compass to determine which direction to travel and to keep you on track as you head to your destination.

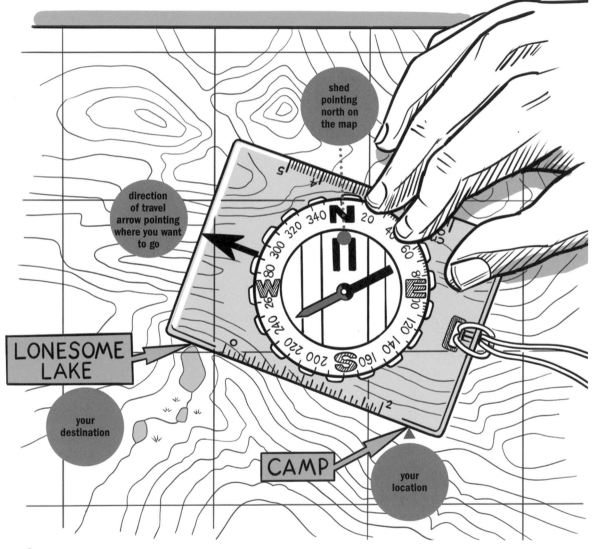

1. **Find your location on the map.** Put the compass on the map with one corner of the baseplate on your current location and the other corner pointing to the place you want to go. Now turn the bezel so that the shed is pointing north on the map. The red needle probably won't be pointing in the same direction, which is fine.

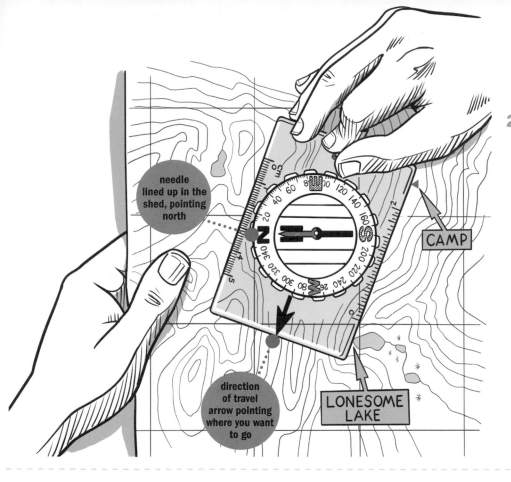

needle lined up in the shed, pointing north

CAMP

direction of travel arrow pointing where you want to go

LONESOME LAKE

2. Holding the map and compass flat, turn until the red needle is lined up with the shed on the disc. Some people call this "Putting red Fred in the shed."

travel direction of arrow

red arrow in shed pointing north

3. Now you can put the map away and use the compass to stay on track. Hold the compass flat in your palm at chest height, keeping the needle within the shed so that it remains pointing north. Follow the direction of travel arrow to find your way to your destination. Check your bearing periodically by making sure the red needle stays in the shed.

Start with your left foot.

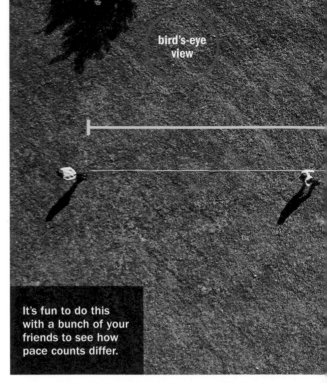

bird's-eye view

It's fun to do this with a bunch of your friends to see how pace counts differ.

MEASURING DISTANCE

Being able to tell how far you've walked helps you determine where you are and how much farther you have to go.

FIGURE OUT YOUR AVERAGE PACE

Your pace is how far you travel when you walk, based on your normal stride. You can use your pace to measure distance.

1. **Starting with your left foot,** walk normally from the beginning to the end of a 100-foot course. Count each time your right foot touches the ground and record that number.

2. **Walk the course** three more times, recording how many times your right foot touches the ground for each cycle.

3. **Add up the four figures,** then divide the sum by 4. This is your average pace count.

Your pace changes with the terrain and the conditions in the environment. To get an accurate idea of what your pace is across a variety of situations, do the above exercise in a flat, open field, a wooded forest, going uphill, going downhill, with your bag fully packed, and with no bag.

WILDERNESS WISDOM
FIND YOUR PACE

First count = 40
Second count = 42
Third count = 41
Fourth count = 41

40 + 42 + 41 + 41 = 164 ÷ 4 =
41 paces per 100 feet

Most maps give distances in both miles and kilometers.

1 mile = 5,280 feet
1 kilometer = 3,281 feet

Walk the course four times.

100 feet

Only count when your right foot hits the ground.

KEEPING TRACK OF DISTANCE

Once you know your average pace, you can use this method to keep track of how far you travel.

1. **Put nine small pebbles** and five larger stones in one pocket. Begin walking and counting your paces. Every time you reach your average pace count, take a small pebble from your full pocket and place it in your empty pocket.

2. **Once you have** moved nine pebbles into the "empty" pocket, you've gone about 900 feet. At the end of your next pace count, place one of the big stones in the same pocket with the nine pebbles. This helps you keep track of when you've gone 1,000 feet (about 333 yards).

3. **Repeat step 2,** transferring the smaller pebble back to your other pocket, and move another large stone for each 1,000 feet you travel.

IF YOU'RE LOST, DON'T LOSE IT

Before you head off alone, always tell someone where you are going and when you plan to be back. If you become disoriented while hiking and find yourself thinking, "I'm sure it's just around the next bend in the trail," or "It must be just over this hill," watch out! Your mind might be playing tricks on you and leading you in the wrong direction. If you do decide that you're lost, the most important thing is to stay calm. Don't panic and start running. This takes you farther away from where you planned to go, which makes it harder for people to find you. You could also get injured.

THE SECRET TO GETTING FOUND

Here's a handy way to remember what to do if you become lost: **STOP**. That stands for Stop, Think, Observe, Plan. Here's what you do:

STOP. Once you realize you're lost, stop moving and make sure you are safe. Take a moment to breathe, relax, and take a drink of water.

THINK. Your brain is your best survival tool. Stay calm and stay where you are while you figure out your next moves. Try to remember where you might have made a wrong turn on the trail and what landmarks you observed.

OBSERVE. What are the current weather conditions? What time of day is it? Where is the best place to set up a shelter? Is it safe to build a fire and is there fuel available? How much food and water do you have?

PLAN. Decide how to best use your resources to stay warm and safe. Figure out how to signal for help.

Now put your plan into action!

Start by blowing your whistle three times in a row, the universal sign for help. Using the whistle takes less energy than yelling. Keep blowing often, even as you implement the rest of your plan.

Build a shelter that will keep you warm and dry in case you can't make a fire.

Create visual aids that can be spotted from a distance and/or from the air:

- Hang something like your emergency blanket.

- Make a large SOS with rocks against a contrasting background.

- Make a big X or an arrow pointing to your camp with branches.

- If it's sunny, use a mirror to signal for help.

SEARCH AREA
+FIRST HOUR+

TIP FROM THE GUIDE
HUNKER DOWN

It's really important to that you stay put once you realize you are lost. You want to keep the search area as small as possible. While firefighters and police officers can sometimes start searching an area very soon after someone is reported missing, full search-and-rescue operations usually take at least 24 hours to set out.

Based on the scale of many topographical maps, the comparative search area is about the size of a business card. If you keep walking, the search area expands very quickly because rescuers don't know which direction you're traveling: within three hours, the search area can be the size of a fully opened newspaper.

USING A KNIFE

Have you ever been mesmerized by the ancient pastime of whittling, fascinated by the repetitive motion of the knife and the chips of wood falling to the ground? Something about this activity seems to connect us with our distant ancestors, who had to make everything they needed. Years ago, lots of people knew how to whittle and often carried a pocketknife with them wherever they went. It's less common today to own a pocketknife and even more rare to know how to use it well.

But when you do know how to use a knife, you can make whatever you need in a wilderness survival situation. This section teaches you how to use a knife safely. You can then practice your knife skills on the carving and woodcraft projects that follow.

TIP FROM THE GUIDE
STATE OF MIND

Be aware of your state of mind before you even touch your knife. Using a knife when you're excited, angry, or upset can lead to accidents. If you are not feeling calm, **STOP**. Pause and take some deep breaths, then ask yourself if you are ready. Take out your knife only when you are centered.

KNIFE SAFETY CONTRACT

A knife is a tool, not a toy, and using one is a privilege. It is your responsibility to take good care of your knife, including making sure it is sharp (see page 53). If you respect your tools, they will be your allies, helping you when you need them to. Use your common sense. If you're wondering whether you should do something with your knife, ask yourself whether it seems safe.

Read the rules listed below (and turn the page for more explanation). Complete the steps on the right to create and sign your knife safety contract before you do anything with your knife.

1. **Trace your hands** on a piece of paper.

2. **Write one safety rule** from the list on each finger.

3. **Explain each rule** to your parent or guardian, making sure they understand each one so they can help you stay safe.

4. **Sign the contract** and have your parent or guardian sign it as well.

BASIC KNIFE RULES

1. Be aware of your environment.
2. Have a clear head.
3. Learn from someone with experience.
4. Draw an imaginary "safety circle."
5. Carve in a safe position.
6. Carve away from yourself.
7. Check for safe follow-through.
8. Always know where your knife is.
9. Store your knife in a safe place.
10. Keep your knife properly sharpened.

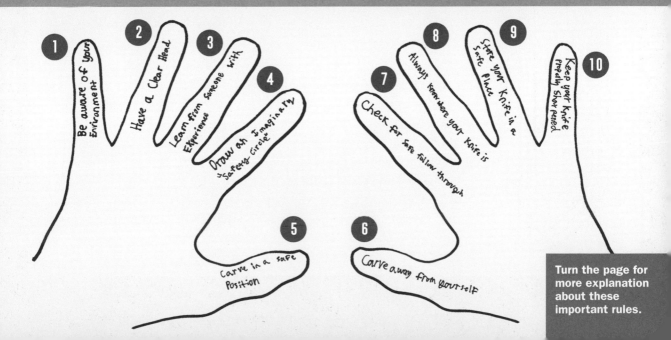

1 Be aware of your Environment
2 Have a Clear Head
3 Learn from someone with Experience
4 Draw an Imaginary "Safety circle"
5 Carve in a safe Position
6 Carve away from yourself
7 Check for safe follow through
8 Always know where your knife is
9 Store your knife in a safe place
10 Keep your knife properly Sharpened

Turn the page for more explanation about these important rules.

KNIFE SAFETY RULES AND BEST PRACTICES

Follow these safety principles any time you use a knife.

1. **Be aware of your environment.** Before you even take out your knife, take a moment to notice what's happening around you: Are you in a safe place? Is there anybody close by? If so, are they running or horsing around?

2. **Have a clear head.** Never use a knife when you're very emotional. If you are sad, angry, or upset, it's easy to be distracted and make mistakes that could hurt you or someone else.

3. **Learn from someone with experience.** These people can bring you back on track by reminding you when your elbow starts to slip off your knees or when you are not paying attention to your carving. Over time you will develop your carving skills and need less supervision.

4. **Draw an imaginary "safety circle"** with your hand that isn't holding the knife. Always be aware of this circle's boundaries and make sure that no one steps into your circle. If anyone even comes close to your circle, sheath your knife right away, safely and without rushing.

5. **Carve in a safe position.** A good one is sitting cross-legged with your elbows on your knees (not your thighs) and leaning forward just a little. Or see the knee-stabilized position on page 44.

6. **Carve away from yourself.** Hold your knife firmly and carve with the blade facing away from your body. You may need to turn the wood as you work to keep your blade in the right position or set the project on a stable surface to support it while you carve.

7. **Check for safe follow-through.** Always consider where the blade will go if it cuts all the way through the wood or slips off your carving. If you get even the slightest feeling that you might cut yourself, **STOP**. You must listen to your inner voice and heed its warning. Adjust your posture and position as necessary.

8. **Always know where your knife is.** Never lay it down, even for a second. If you are carving a project, hold your knife in your hand. If you are taking a break, secure the knife in its sheath. Do *not* stick it in a piece of wood.

9. **Store your knife in a safe place.** Protect yourself and the people in your life when you're not using your knife. For example, even though you should have your knife with you when you are out on an adventure, if you are running through the woods or hiking along a trail, keep your knife inside your pack until you are ready to use it. Make sure you have a special place to store your knife where it can't be reached by someone who doesn't know how to use it.

10. **Keep your knife properly sharpened.** A dull knife is dangerous. If you are using your knife properly, it should slice through wood very easily. If you have to push or put a lot of pressure on your carving stroke, it means your knife blade is either dull or jagged. This can be very dangerous because you have to increase the force you use, and if you slip while carving, you can cut yourself badly. Using a knife with a jagged blade also rips the wood, which dulls the blade even more rapidly while leaving microscopic pieces of metal in the wood. (See page 53 to learn how to properly sharpen a knife.)

GET A GRIP

There are different ways to hold a knife depending on what kind of cut you want to make and what material you are cutting into. Here are the knife grips you will use the most.

Your thumb should be wrapped around your knuckles and the blade of the knife should be pointing away from your palm.

Forward grip. This is the easiest, most commonsense grip and the one that you'll use the most. Take your knife out of its sheath and hold it in your dominant hand as you would hold on to bicycle handlebars. Do *not* put your thumb on the back of the blade in the forward grip.

When holding the knife in front of you in the reverse grip, the blade points directly back at you.

Reverse grip. This is the opposite of the forward grip, with the knife blade pointing toward your palm. Use this grip to cut rope or harvest roots or grass. Carefully pull the knife toward you, making sure you have a safe follow-through, meaning that if the knife slips off your carving, your body will not be in danger.

Chest lever grip. Starting with the knife in a forward grip, rotate the edge of the knife so it's in line with your top knuckles. Place your thumb on the face of the blade and hold the object you are carving in your opposite hand. With both hands placed firmly on your chest and the blade pointing away from you, make a scissorlike motion using both hands equally to cut through the piece. If you don't apply even force with both hands, this technique will not work. You can also expand your chest forward to get more power.

This is a very powerful grip that gives you a lot of strength and force.

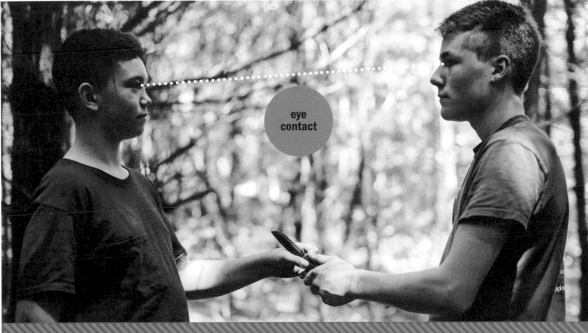

eye contact

TIP FROM THE GUIDE

PASSING THE KNIFE

1. Holding the knife in a forward grip, extend your arm out to the person receiving your knife.

2. Holding on to the neck of the handle with your index finger and thumb, let go with your other three fingers.

3. Angle the handle of the knife toward the other person's outstretched hand and make eye contact with that person.

4. When the other person has taken hold of the handle, say, "Thank you," and release the knife. You have now transferred your blade handle safely into someone else's hand.

LEARNING KNIFE SKILLS

It's good to know a few basic cuts that you can use to make items for your campsite. Here are a few to practice. As with any new skill, carving takes a lot of practice. Start by getting used to how the knife feels in your hand and how the blade feels moving through the wood.

A knife is intended to slice in a manner similar to how a samurai uses a sword. The secret is having a fluid stroke without putting too much effort or muscle into the movement. You want the blade to glide smoothly along the wood, with an angle similar to when you peel a cucumber or carrot.

SAFE POSITION

Always carve in a position that allows for safe follow-through. The **knee-stabilized position** shown here is good for controlled carving. Lock your wrist against your raised knee with the blade facing out. Hold it steady so it does not move. Position the wood against the knife blade at the position and angle you want to cut. Rather than pushing the blade into the wood, pull the wood against the blade to make your cut.

POWER CUT

This is a standard carving cut. Start with the heel of the blade against the object you are carving. Holding the wood firmly, apply pressure on your knife to make an arcing cut that uses the entire blade.

THUMB-ASSIST CUT

This technique is helpful for fine detail work. Start with the knife in a forward grip. Use the thumb of your opposite hand to apply pressure to the spine of the blade as you pull the wood against it. The hand holding the knife is just maintaining control and placing the blade exactly where you want it (not pushing the knife forward).

ROSE PETAL CUT

This cut is useful when you need to cut a branch into lengths with your knife — for example, when cutting up kindling or making a walking staff (see page 118). It works best with branches less than 2 inches in diameter. The idea is to weaken the fibers by cutting into the core to so you can snap the branch.

1. Holding your blade at a 45-degree angle, make a cut about one-third to halfway into the wood. Spin the branch slightly and repeat.

2. Do this five times total (roses have five petals, hence the name). When you snap the branch, the cuts create a slightly rounded tip.

TIP FROM THE GUIDE
CARVING MISTAKES

Don't worry or get frustrated if you make a lot of mistakes at first. Keep things in perspective and realize that learning to carve takes a lot of practice! Here are two common mistakes to try to avoid.

Plowing is when you push a single part of the knife blade against the wood instead of moving the whole blade through the cut. Doing so can quickly dull the blade in that spot.

Angling the knife too deeply causes the blade to dig into the wood, which prevents a fluid carving motion. Trying to force the blade is dangerous. Instead, pull it out and start again at a better angle.

STOP CUT WITH NOTCH

A stop cut is a carving technique for making more controlled cuts. It stops your blade from going too far when you make a second cut. Use it for making notches, as shown on these pages, or a spoon (see page 125).

1. Using the forward grip, hold the blade against the stick and rock it back and forth to make a cut one-quarter to one-third of the way into the stick. This is the stop cut.

2. Make a small slice into the cut to take off a layer of bark.

3. Slice down to the stop cut by holding the knife steady and pulling the branch against the blade.

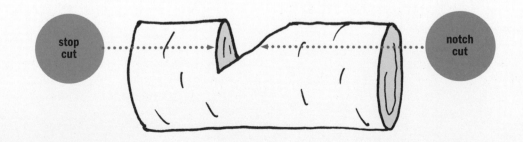

4. Carefully shave off several more layers, cutting at a slight angle to create a shallow notch.

stop cut

notch cut

POT HOOK NOTCH

Use this deep notch to create a hook that can hold a cookpot over your campfire (see page 98). Start with a stick 1 to 1½ inches thick.

1. Hold the blade at a 45-degree angle across the grain of the stick, a few inches from the end. Using the power cut grip (see page 44), rock the knife gently back and forth on the wood to make a cut ⅓ to ½ inch deep.

2. Change the angle of the blade and repeat step 1 to create an X across the first cut.

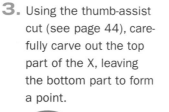

3. Using the thumb-assist cut (see page 44), carefully carve out the top part of the X, leaving the bottom part to form a point.

Cut away this part.

Leave this point.

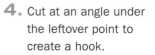

4. Cut at an angle under the leftover point to create a hook.

Don't cut off the tip of the point!

CARVING A HOLE

Carving a hole in a stick comes in handy when you want to feed a rope through a stick, for making a bow drill for starting a fire, or for making traps for hunting and fishing. Use a stick about 1 inch thick.

1. Using the forward grip, carve a shallow V about one-quarter of the way into the wood. Turn the stick to move back and forth to make the V even on both sides. This is called a "saddle notch," because when you're done, it looks like the seat of a saddle.

2. Flip the stick over and repeat step 1 to create a saddle notch opposite the first one.

3. Carefully holding the blade with your forefinger, middle finger, and thumb, use the tip to mark a small rectangle at the narrow part where the notches meet. Flip the stick over and mark another rectangle. Cut into the lines, flipping the stick back and forth a few times to work from both sides, until you can pop out the rectangle to create the hole.

BAToNING

Batoning is a technique for splitting pieces of wood by striking the spine of your knife with another piece of wood called a baton. The baton gives you more power and lets you use your knife like an axe. Use this technique to make kindling or to square off a large branch or log to make a flat surface.

Make a baton by evening off the ends of a thick branch that fits comfortably in your hand and is about the length of your forearm. You also need a flat, stable cutting surface made of wood, such as a large log with a section cut out of it. This is to protect your blade when you reach the end of the cut.

- -

TROUBLESHOOTING

The thicker the wood you are trying to split, the harder it gets, so start by practicing with pieces that are 2 to 3 inches thick.

With thicker pieces, start your split off from the center of the wood so your knife is less likely to get stuck.

If the blade does get stuck, it might have hit a knot in the wood. To loosen it, carefully push down on the knife handle, then pull up gently. Continue rocking the blade to free it. Start your cut in a different spot to get past the knot.

WARNING

To baton safely, you need to use a sheath knife with at least a three-quarter tang. Do **not** use a lock blade knife for batoning. A lock blade knife has moving parts and a mechanism that lets it fold. A folding knife isn't stable or strong enough for batoning.

1. Hold your knife in a forward grip (see page 42). Stand your piece of wood on the cutting surface. Place the blade sharp-side down into the end of the wood.

2. Using the baton, strike the middle of the spine of the knife. This will set your blade.

3. Gently tap the baton on the spine of the knife to set the blade deeper into the wood.

4. Maintain pressure on the knife handle, keeping it straight up and down. Do not twist the knife. Keep the blade in the same level position with every blow. Continue striking the spine of the knife blade, avoiding hitting the tip, until the wood splits.

edge
test

TRY THE PAPER TEST

To figure out if your knife needs to be sharpened, try this simple test. You can also try this after a sharpening session to make sure you've done a good job.

1. Hold a piece of paper securely with one hand.

2. Use the knife to slice through a corner of the paper. A sharp knife should make a clean cut.

3. If the paper tears or catches, there is a dull spot on your blade. You can't just sharpen that spot, though. You have to sharpen the whole blade every time.

SHARPENING YOUR KNIFE

In a survival situation, conserving energy is important. Your knife needs to be sharp so you can use it effectively. For best results, use a sharpening stone that has a coarse-to-medium-grit side and a fine-grit side. If your knife is jagged or misshapen, or if it ripped the paper when you tried the paper test (see page 52), start with the coarse side. If your knife is new or you regularly maintain it, you can use the fine-grit side to touch up your blade, as shown here.

When the bevel is held correctly against the stone, the spine will be slightly lifted.

1. Place the stone on a sturdy surface with the fine-grit side facing up. Position the knife blade on the stone facing away from you and at the same angle as the blade's bevel.

2. Push the knife across the stone, moving the blade away from you. Use firm pressure to move the entire blade, from heel to tip, across the entire stone, keeping the face of the bevel on the stone and the spine slightly lifted. Do not drag the blade.

3. The number of strokes depends on how much sharpening the blade needs. The important thing is to keep count, because you will make the same number of strokes on both sides.

4. Turn your knife over and repeat step 2 on the other face of the blade. Always make the same number of strokes on each side of the blade.

5. As you sharpen the blade, the metal at the very edge becomes so thin that it folds over, creating a microscopic bend along the blade. This is called the "burr." To check for the burr, carefully feel the very edge of the knife with your fingernail (not the pad of your thumb!), moving away from the blade.

6. Stroking the edge of the blade against a leather belt is called "stropping." The action takes off the burr and makes a really sharp edge. Secure one end of the belt, with the rough side of the leather facing up, to something that won't move. Slowly drag just the edge of the blade in one direction, moving from heel to toe as when you used the stone. Don't let the side or back of the blade touch the leather. Flip the blade and bring it back along the strap on the other side. Do this several times, flipping the blade each time and being sure to use the entire blade.

BUILDING A FIRE

Humans have been making fire for more than a million years, so it is no wonder that a campfire transports us back in time. Knowing how to make a fire is one of the most important survival skills you can learn. As you master this skill, adopt the right mind-set. Before you even pick up the tools to build a fire, picture the fire in your mind's eye and trust that you have the ability to make that fire. The more you believe in your abilities, the more successful you'll be.

SAFETY FIRST

Building a fire is a serious responsibility and requires paying attention to a few important rules. Area wildlife, nearby homes, or your own life may depend on your abilities.

Before you choose a spot, consider safety, safety, safety! When you're in the woods, don't build a fire where the layers of leaf litter and duff are dry and thick, or on top of tree roots. Leaf litter is the top layer of leaves, pine needles, and such found on the forest floor; duff is the layer of decomposing organic material under the litter. These materials could easily ignite and cause a wildfire. A fire built over tree roots can eventually burn down and ignite the entire tree (see page 60).

Weather conditions are another important part of fire making. Several factors — including the outside temperature, wind speeds, and how dry the ground is — influence the fire danger level. Always check conditions with the local fire department or park service.

When you build a fire, keep water nearby so you can extinguish it at any point. Don't build a fire bigger than you need it to be for cooking and keeping warm. Finally, never leave a fire, or even the embers, unattended.

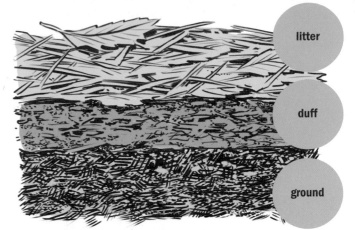

litter

duff

ground

FIRE SAFETY RULES

- Choose your location carefully, avoiding root systems and thick duff.
- Be aware of weather conditions.
- Always dig a firepit to contain your fire.
- Only make a fire as big as you need.
- Have water nearby for putting out your fire.
- Never leave a fire unattended.

DIGGING A FIREPIT

It's important to build a firepit to contain your fire and make it easier to control. You should dig some type of pit every time you make a fire in a new location. These directions are for making a large firepit when you'll be camping in one spot for a few days.

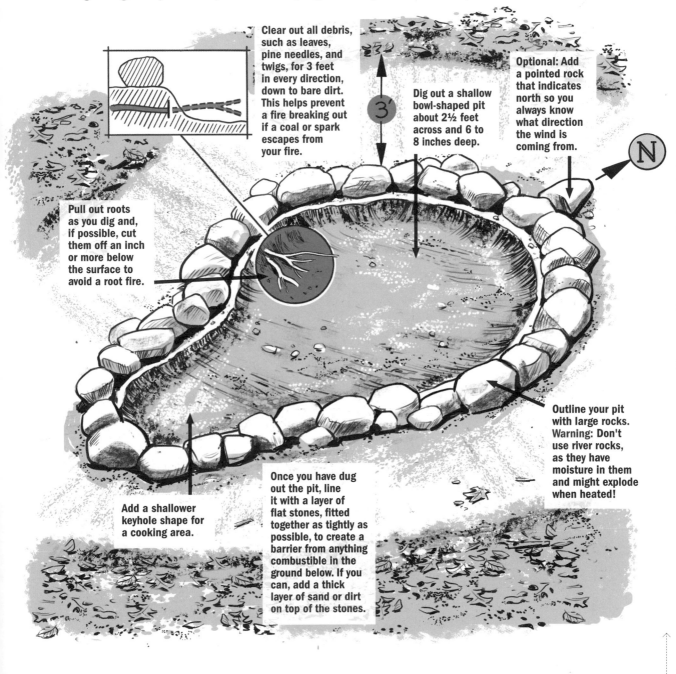

Clear out all debris, such as leaves, pine needles, and twigs, for 3 feet in every direction, down to bare dirt. This helps prevent a fire breaking out if a coal or spark escapes from your fire.

Dig out a shallow bowl-shaped pit about 2½ feet across and 6 to 8 inches deep.

Optional: Add a pointed rock that indicates north so you always know what direction the wind is coming from.

N

3'

Pull out roots as you dig and, if possible, cut them off an inch or more below the surface to avoid a root fire.

Outline your pit with large rocks. Warning: Don't use river rocks, as they have moisture in them and might explode when heated!

Add a shallower keyhole shape for a cooking area.

Once you have dug out the pit, line it with a layer of flat stones, fitted together as tightly as possible, to create a barrier from anything combustible in the ground below. If you can, add a thick layer of sand or dirt on top of the stones.

DIGGING A FIREPIT continued

Root fires start when the ends of the roots become embers. The fire then travels underground along the roots and through the duff layer, popping up in fuel pockets, such as piles of leaves or pine needles. Then the fire comes out at the base of shrubs and trees, and travels up the trunks and branches. No matter what kind of forest you are in, **always** build your firepit so that the embers will have no contact with roots or fine rootlets.

TIP FROM THE GUIDE
DUE NORTH

When you're building your firepit, place a large, pointed stone on the north side of your ring. That way, at any moment, you can look at the firepit and have your bearings.

Knowing your direction also helps keep you oriented to changes in the wind. The action of the smoke as it rises, swirls around, or blows in different directions, can tell you that the air pressure is changing, perhaps bringing changes in the weather.

FIRE VOCABULARY

TINDER is a general term for dried fibrous material — such as cattail down, grasses, goldenrod, inner tree bark, grapevine, leaf litter, pine needles, and ferns — that can be used to start a fire.

KINDLING is small, woody material that ignites into a strong flame when you hold burning tinder to it for five seconds. Kindling can be as thick as a pencil or your finger. Conifers have a resin that can help light and establish a fire.

FUEL is what keeps the fire burning once it's started. As your fire grows, you can add bigger sticks and then logs. Gather a good supply of dry fuel before you make a fire. Look for pieces about as thick as your arm and no thicker than your leg.

HEAT is necessary to ignite the fuel. You can get heat from a number of sources, including matches, a ferro rod, or two sticks rubbed together.

OXYGEN keeps the fire burning. Fanning with your hand or blowing with your breath will help ignite the tinder and get the kindling burning. But be careful — too much oxygen will blow your fire out.

MAKING A TWIG BUNDLE

Many live trees have dead branches that make excellent kindling. A twig bundle is a good way to start a fire if you are in a forest with hemlocks or similar conifers that tend to have short, dry, dead sticks. Collect twigs from trees, not ones from the ground, which will be damp.

It's a good idea to make several twig bundles at once, so you have a supply of them on hand in your camp.

Two bundles are good for starting most fires; make them bigger if you're making a fire in damp conditions.

1. Look for twigs about the thickness of a pencil and about the length of your arm. Only collect ones that snap off easily and crack loudly when you break them. Very bendy ones are still green on the inside and won't burn.

TIP FROM THE GUIDE
GATHER WISELY

Don't break branches or peel the bark off live trees. Trying to burn wood that hasn't been dead for a long time is difficult. More importantly, you don't want to damage living trees.

2. Gather a large handful of twigs. Arrange them so that all of the thicker ends are together.

3. Holding the thicker ends of the twigs in one hand, grab the smaller ends with your other hand and twist or bend them until they break off. This will be your tinder that lights the twig bundle. You can also use dry ferns, birch bark, or pine needles as tinder.

4. Fold the remaining bundle in half to create a bend. (It's okay if the twigs snap.)

5. Push the small pile of tinder into the bent end of the twig bundle. (If the twigs broke when you bent them, just stuff the tinder into the middle of the twigs at one end.)

6. Wrap the bundle with a long piece of grass, a strip of bark, or a piece of cordage (see page 130), and tie it tightly.

STRIKE IT RIGHT

Striking a match might seem like a simple thing, but to make sure you can get a strong flame when you really need to make a fire, it's important to practice beforehand. When it's cold and wet and maybe you're lost, getting a fire going could save your life. Practice this technique with strong wooden kitchen matches. Keep trying until you can do it consistently.

Hold the match with your middle finger and thumb gripping just under the head and your index finger at the end of the stick. Using this grip makes it less likely that the match will break.

With a swift downward motion, strike the match against the box at a 45-degree angle. As soon as the match ignites, adjust your grip so that you are holding the end of the match between your index finger and thumb. Use your other three fingers to shield the flame from the wind.

USING A FERRO ROD

A ferro rod can create thousands of fires. See page 19 to learn more.

Hold the rod firmly in one hand while pointing it at your tinder. Place the scraper at a 45-degree angle to the rod.

Pull the rod sharply toward yourself while pressing hard with the scraper. Do this several times. Direct the sparks at your tinder, being careful not to scatter it as you strike the rod.

LIGHTING A FIRE

Before you light a fire, gather plenty of fuel (see page 62). You want to have enough to keep your fire going for a while. Make a few twig bundles, then use this procedure to light a fire.

1. Instead of lighting a fire on the ground, which is often moist and cold, hold the twig bundle in your hand to ignite it, allowing it to establish a strong flame before you place it in the firepit. Turn the bundle so that the finest tinder is facing down, and apply the match to the bottom of the bundle.

2. Once the tinder catches, keep the bundle level, adjusting your hold so the flame moves up to catch the thicker sticks.

See page 123 for another cool way to get a fire going.

3. When you have a steady flame, lay the twig bundle in the firepit. Place pencil- to wrist-size sticks on top of the burning bundle. Don't pile them up too thickly; remember, a fire needs oxygen to burn. Light and add another twig bundle or two if needed.

4. If necessary, blow on the fire to make it stronger, but only after there are some burning embers. You don't want to blow out the flame!

5. Add more wood as the fire becomes established. Start with small branches, piling them in different directions to let air in. Once those are burning, you can add bigger logs, always being careful not to add too much at once so you don't smother the flames.

WARNING
Never leave a fire unattended, even after it dies down to embers.

EXTINGUISHING A FIRE

Before you leave your campsite, it's very important that you make sure your fire is **completely out**. Once the flames have burned down to embers, here's what you do.

1. Find a couple of branches or poles, 2 to 3 inches thick and 3 to 4 feet long. Cut the thicker end of one branch to create a flat tamping surface. Whittle the end of the other branch into a point, if it isn't already pointed.

2. Use the flat end of the stick to pound on the embers, breaking them into smaller and smaller pieces.

3. Stab the pointed stick into the ground to make holes where water can collect under the embers and saturate the ground. *You don't need to do step 3 in a pit lined with rocks, only in a less-permanent firepit.*

4. Pour a bucket of water in a slow stream from overhead so the water goes through the embers to saturate the ground. Stir the embers again and keep pouring additional buckets of water until no more steam comes up.

5. Keep stirring, stabbing, and pouring until the ashes are cool enough to touch.

TIP FROM THE GUIDE

WITH GREAT POWER COMES GREAT RESPONSIBILITY

Spider-Man may have popularized this saying, but it's incredibly relevant and important when dealing with fire. Fire is a powerful force that consumes anything in its path and transforms it into heat and energy. A smoldering campfire that's not extinguished properly can quickly grow into a raging forest fire.

TYING KNOTS

Tying sturdy, reliable knots is one of the most useful and valuable skills you can develop if you plan to spend a lot of time outdoors. With knots, you can make sure your campsite is weathertight, make a fishing net, keep your gear secure, and make tools. All of these are things of beauty, to be sure, but that's not all. Being able to tie a good knot goes a long way toward ensuring safety, comfort, and enjoyment.

overhand
on a bight

KNOT-TYING TERMINOLOGY

A knot is a fastening made with string, rope, or cord. It is used to attach the cord to another object, such as a tree, the corner of a tarp, or another piece of cord. Knots can be temporary and easy to release, or sturdy and meant for long-term or even permanent hold. A knot that fails because it isn't properly tied is said to capsize, collapse, or spill.

The good news is you don't need an encyclopedic knowledge of this subject to get rocking! Being able to work a few primary knots will let you do everything you need to do in the wilderness — and give you a start in understanding and learning more complicated knots. Using the proper terms will help you learn this great skill.

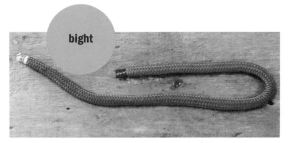

Knot. A knot is used to join two pieces of rope.

Bight. A bend in the line anywhere between the ends. Often in a U shape, a bight can point up, down, or sideways.

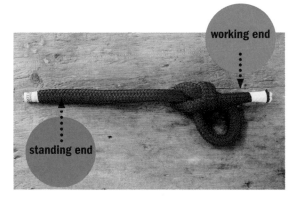

Ends. Each cord has two ends; these are where the cord is trimmed and sealed. The working end of the cord is actively involved in making the knot. The standing end, sometimes called the "bitter end," is the part of the cord not engaged with either making the knot or having something turned or tied around it.

Hitch. A knot that attaches the cord to another object, such as a ring or a post.

MUST-KNOW KNOTS

The following knots are both fundamental and versatile. Whether you use just one by itself or a few of them together, these will provide a true foundation for developing strong knot-tying skills.

OVERHAND ON A BIGHT

This basic knot can come in handy for a variety of situations and projects, including hanging equipment and setting up tarps.

1. Bend your cord to make a bight — an open loop a few inches long.

2. Pinch the end of the bight and fold the tip back over the standing end of the cord to form a circle.

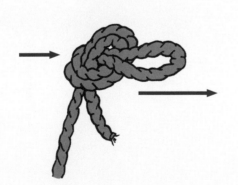

3. Pass the bight under and back up through the circle.

4. Pull it tight to make the knot, leaving the end of the bight sticking out to make a closed loop.

overhand on a bight

You can use this knot to attach a cord to a tarp or, as shown here, to hang your pack or other equipment.

FRICTION WRAP WITH HALF HITCHES

This is one of the fastest and strongest methods of securing the end of a rope to a fixed point. You can practice it inside with a table or chair leg or outside with a fence post or tree trunk.

1. Wrap a length of cord fully around the object twice.

2. Pass the working end of the cord over, then back under the standing end of the cord, to form a "half hitch."

3. Add a second half hitch by bringing the working end back under, then over, the standing end again, keeping it in front of your first half hitch.

4. Slide the knot up the working end of the cord to tighten it and keep it in place. The magic of this knot is that the rope is held in place by friction. The half hitches are for added security; they don't hold any weight.

Use the clove hitch to make a tripod for cooking (see page 96).

CLOVE HITCH

This strong hitch can bear a heavy load and is a useful way to temporarily connect something at a right angle to an anchor point.

1. Pass the working end of the cord around a branch or post.

2. Bring the working end around the branch again and form an X with the standing end of the cord.

Pinch here.

Thread under the X here.

3. Pinch the X to hold it in place, and pass the working end around the post again. Thread the working end under and through the X.

4. Pull enough cord through the X to form a "tail" that you can pull tight to secure.

TRUCKER'S HITCH

Use the trucker's hitch for a stable line that can support a tarp or bags of food.

This two-part, or compound, knot acts like a pulley system so you can tighten it as much as you need. It's a very strong hitch and is one of the most valuable knots to master.

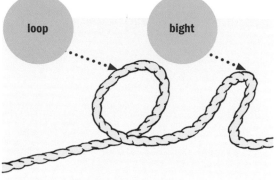

1. Attach one end of the cord to a fixed point, such as a sturdy tree, using a friction wrap.

2. Pull the cord out to a second fixed point. Create a small loop in the cord, then make a bight a short distance up the cord.

3. Pass the bight through the loop and pull it tight, forming a new secure loop.

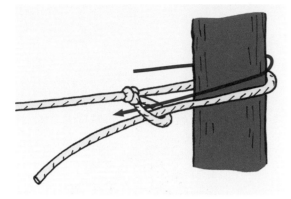 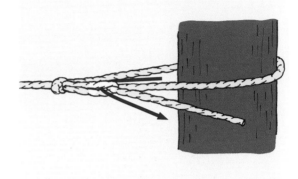

4. Take the working end of the cord and pass it around the tree at the height you want your line to be. Pass the working end through the loop.

5. Pull the working end back toward the tree. You will feel and see the cord tighten and put pressure on the cord. Pull through as much tension as you need.

6. Once the cord is tight enough, bring the working end back toward the tree. Pinch where the loop and working end cross to keep it tight. Now tie two half hitches with the working end to secure the hitch in place.

TAUT-LINE HITCH

This adjustable loop knot secures your rope to a fixed object when the cord is put under tension. One use for it is setting up an A-frame shelter (see page 102).

1. Loop your cord around a strong tree or post, and cross the working end over the standing end.

2. Loop the working end back over the cord and coil it around the standing end two times.

3. Bring the working end up to make a half hitch on the outside of the coils.

4. Cinch the knot tightly to secure it and slide the knot up and down the cord to tighten or loosen the line.

MARLINSPIKE HITCH

This is a quick and easy knot that attaches to a stick to form a handle. You can use it to hang up your gear or a hammock with a toggle (see page 93).

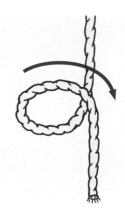

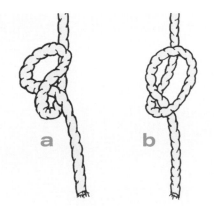

1. Make a loop in your cord.

2. Twist the loop to form a bight (**a**). Line the bight up over the standing end of the cord (**b**).

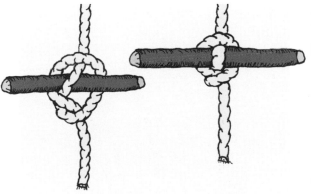

3. Pull the standing end of the cord forward through the bight and slide your toggle between the standing cord and the bight.

4. Pull the ends of the cord tight over the toggle to secure it.

ROPE STORAGE

At the end of a great adventure, it is really easy (especially if you're tired) to get sloppy with your equipment and just stuff it away. "I'll take care of it later," you might say, thinking you won't need your gear again immediately. But I promise you, it's better to take a few minutes to properly store your ropes at the end of your outing than to discover the next time you really need a rope that you are the owner of a horrible mess. Few things are more discouraging than a tangled wreck at a desperate moment. And, at the same time, it is a true pleasure when a well-kept line feeds out perfectly.

BUTTERFLY HANK

This is a quick way to tie up lengths of paracord and other thin rope to keep it all neat and organized for easy storage.

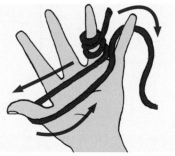

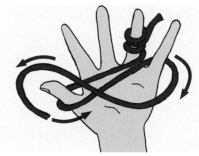

1. Wrap the end of the cord around your ring finger a few times to secure it. Keeping your fingers spread wide apart, wrap the cord around your thumb, then bring it back across your palm to your pinky.

2. Loop the cord around the inside of your pinky and bring it back to your thumb, crossing over to form an X, or a figure 8, against your palm.

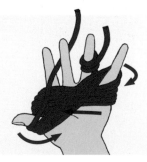

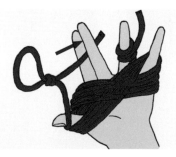

3. Continue looping the cord back and forth around your thumb and pinky in alternating directions to build up the shape of the figure 8 with the cord.

4. When you have a few inches of cord remaining, with the working end around the underside of your thumb, pinch the working end between your index and middle finger. Form a loop and twist it twice.

5. Slide the bundle of cord off your thumb and bring the twisted loop over the bundle to the middle of the figure 8.

6. Tighten the loop around the cord bundle. This will form a "button" that holds it securely.

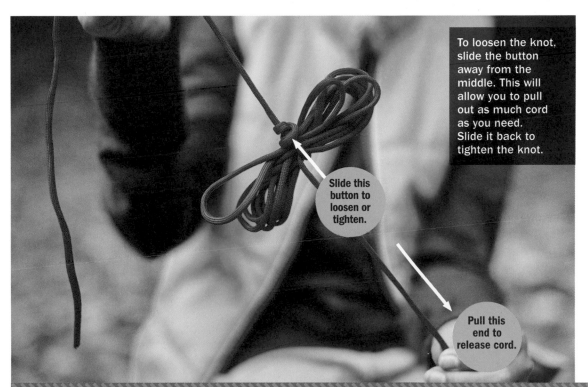

To loosen the knot, slide the button away from the middle. This will allow you to pull out as much cord as you need. Slide it back to tighten the knot.

Slide this button to loosen or tighten.

Pull this end to release cord.

TIP FROM THE GUIDE
PRACTICE, PRACTICE, PRACTICE

You've learned LOTS of useful skills in this chapter. Now you have to practice them. Take and make any excuse to do so. Watching TV? Have a little cordage on hand and try tying knots. Stuck watching your little brother? Make a tarp "fort." When the weather is cold and wet, go outside and see what it's like to make knots when you and your rope are soaked through. Practice in the dark. Practice when you have an injury that's forcing you to stay off your feet.

A survival situation might include the very worst possible conditions; that's why it's called survival. So test yourself and hone your skills before you're out in the wild. Then, if you ever do really *need* these skills, you'll be able to push through and discover the hero that lives inside you!

3

SETTING UP CAMP

Now that you know what equipment you need and have practiced and become proficient at some important survival skills, it's time for you to answer the call to adventure. In this chapter, you'll learn how to set up your very own campsite. The time is now. Your adventure awaits!

CHOOSE YOUR LOCATION

Before setting up your camp, always get permission or a permit, as required. Make sure you understand the laws and regulations in effect where you are; these could be very different depending on whether you're on private land or in a state or national park.

There are many factors to consider when choosing a campsite. Here are some of the most important ones. Choose a spot that:

- **Isn't on wet, soggy ground** or in a low-lying area that might harbor mosquitoes or flood if it rains heavily

- **Allows fresh air to circulate** and clear away smoke and humid air

- **Isn't on a high,** exposed area where wind, rain, and lightning could be a problem

- **Has easy access** to adequate firewood and water

- **Has enough open space** for you to set up eating and sleeping areas, safely build a firepit, and dig pits for food and waste disposal

---

TIP FROM THE GUIDE

LOOK UP!

When you find a clearing that meets your needs, spend some time looking overhead for what are called "widow-makers" — large broken branches that are dangling above the ground, or entire dead trees that might fall over. They are a hazard because you never know when they might become dislodged by wind or rain and fall. Set up your camp at least 100 feet away from any hazards that you see.

A LIST OF THINGS TO LOOK OUT FOR

Here are some more details you should pay attention to when choosing a campsite:

- **Wood.** You need wood for your fire, but also to build a shelter (see page 101), so look for broken branches on the ground, dead trees, and species like hemlock that provide good tinder.

- **Water.** You should carry plenty of drinking water with you while hiking, but you'll need more for cooking, washing up, and putting out your fire. Experienced explorers always plan their routes around access to water.

- **Man-made hazards.** In some parts of the country, forested areas cover old farms, where people used to bury their trash in dumps. Watch out for barbed wire, rusty metal, broken glass, and other junk.

- **Natural hazards.** Learn to identify plants to avoid, like poison ivy, poison oak, and hogweed. Look for yellow jacket or ground bee nests. Notice if there are a lot of mosquitoes, gnats, or flies around.

- **Signs of wildlife.** One of the great things about camping is learning about animals, birds, and insects, but always remember you're a visitor in their homes. Be a respectful guest. Learn to notice trails that deer or other animals use frequently or that might be near an animal den, then choose a camping site that gives wild neighbors the space they need. This is also a matter of your own safety. See more about being aware of bears on page 95.

lightning strike

It is a total myth that lightning never strikes the same place twice, so if you see a tree with lightning damage, build your camp somewhere else.

ground wasp nest

sign of bear

ORGANIZE YOUR CAMPSITE

Once you have chosen a location for your campsite, there are a few tasks you should do right away to make sure you get the most out of your camping experience.

Hang tarps for cover.

Gather firewood.

Create some seating.

Dig a firepit.

Stow your gear.

Set up a kitchen area.

CAMPSITE CHECKLIST

If you plan to use a site for more than a few days or to return to it again and again, you can set up a more permanent camp.

Collect a supply of firewood.

This "tool tree" is made by cutting off a few low, evenly spaced branches.

- **Make a firepit area** (see page 59). Choose an open spot and clear all debris and brush for 3 feet in all directions.

- **Find a spot to sleep.** Scout out a good place to pitch your tent or A-frame tarp shelter (see page 102) or build a cozy debris hut (see page 108).

- **Collect a supply of firewood.** Designate an area where you can break up long sticks and cut firewood without interfering with other activities.

- **Create some cover.** Hang tarps over your firewood area, kitchen site, and anywhere else you want to provide shelter from rain.

- **Set up a kitchen area.** You will need enough room to store food and cooking gear, and prepare meals. Think about cleanup, too (see page 97 for more about that). When camping in bear country, your kitchen and sleeping areas should be at least 200 feet apart. See pages 96 and 98 for simple projects that will make cooking easier.

- **Designate a water area.** You need a supply of water for washing hands, cooking, and extinguishing your fire. See page 140 for ideas on collecting water.

TIP FROM THE GUIDE

ORGANIZE YOUR TOOLS

If you are setting up a semipermanent adventure camp like the one shown here, you will have all kinds of equipment — a shovel to dig out your firepit, plus saws and knives for various projects — and it's best to keep all your tools consolidated in one area. This way everything is in one place and you'll always know where to look for a tool. When you're done using each tool, return it to that spot. This will help prevent your tools from getting left in a debris pile or outside of camp.

HANG YOUR GEAR

Hanging your pack at chest level keeps it off of damp ground and allows you easy access to your gear. Use a tree that is at least 3 inches in diameter. You'll need to make a toggle for your pack first (see page 93).

1. Cut a piece of paracord about the length of your arm span. Make an overhand bight on one end.

2. Wrap the paracord around the tree and thread the working end through the loop. Cinch the paracord tightly around the tree.

3. With the standing end of the paracord, make a marlinspike around the toggle.

4. Bring the toggle through the handle at the top of the pack and let the pack hang.

MAKE A TOGGLE

A toggle is a short, sturdy stick that is handy for hanging your pack and other gear. Making one is a good way to practice your carving skills.

WHAT YOU NEED

- A piece of wood, about ½ inch thick and 4–6 inches long
- A knife

WHAT YOU DO

Round off the ends of the wood using a rose petal cut (see page 45). Leave the bark on, peel it off completely, or create a design by carefully carving away only some of the bark.

Use your carving skills to decorate your toggle and make it recognizably yours.

SETTING UP A SAFE KITCHEN

Locate your cooking and food storage area well away from your sleeping area. Many animals are attracted by the smell of food and other human scents, like toothpaste, which they associate with food. Smaller animals, like mice, squirrels, and raccoons, might nibble on your equipment or spoil your food supplies, but bears are dangerous when they are looking for food. You don't want a bear poking into your tent because it smells like dinner!

When camping in bear country, place your cooking area at least 200 feet away from your sleeping area. After you cook and eat, change your clothes or smoke them thoroughly by the fire before you go to your sleeping area.

Store your food by hanging it between two trees. Or buy a specially designed bear-proof canister. **Note:** Some parks require these canisters. Others provide bear poles or special storage caches at campsites. Check the rules before you set out.

BE THE CAMP CHEF

In your kitchen at home, you can set the oven temperature to bake or broil and adjust the stove burners with the twist of a knob depending on whether you want a simmer or a boil. To be a good camp chef, you need to be able to create a consistent level of heat with your fires. The secret lies in using hardwood, which burns slower, lasts longer, and throws more uniform heat than softwood does. Good wood for cooking fires comes from beech, birch, ash, juniper, cottonwood, willow, and oak trees.

It may look like more fun to cook over an open flame, but a bed of embers works better for even cooking. After the fire in the main part of your firepit burns down, rake the embers into the keyhole area. See page 144 for some great recipes to try out.

MAKING A BEAR HANG

MINIMUM
6'

8-10'

To hang your food out of reach of bears and other critters, you need a stuff sack or two to hold the food, about 20 feet of paracord or other narrow rope, a carabiner (optional but handy), and some sort of weight, like a half-full water bottle or small stuff sack with a few rocks inside.

Find a tree at least 200 feet away from your sleeping area that has a branch you can toss a rope over. You want your bag hanging 8 to 10 feet off the ground, so the branch has to be higher than that, but not too high to throw the rope over.

- Tie the water bottle or other weight to one end of the line.

- Throw the weight over the branch so that the line hangs several feet from the trunk. This might take a few attempts!

- Remove the weight and tie the food bag onto the end of the line with a couple of half hitches or use a carabiner to clip it in place. Pull the bag into the air at least 8 feet high.

- Tie off the loose end of the line by wrapping it around another tree trunk or branch, or a large rock or log on the ground, or whatever method works for your situation. You don't need a fancy knot. Just be sure the line is secure.

COOKING TRIPOD

Set up a tripod over your firepit so that you can hang a pot of water or food directly over the fire.

WHAT YOU NEED

- 3 straight poles, 6–10 feet long and 2–3 inches in diameter
- About 12 feet of paracord

WHAT YOU DO

1. Lay the branches on the ground in a row with a couple of inches between them. Tie a clove hitch (see page 76) around the one closest to you, about a foot from the end, and pull it snug.

2. Weave the working end of the paracord back and forth, under and over the branches, leaving some room between them. You don't want them to be tied too tightly. Make five or six passes with the paracord.

3. Wrap the remaining cord once around the joints between the branches. Finish off with another clove hitch.

4. Set the tripod up over your firepit, making sure it is well balanced.

tripod

pot hook
(see page 98)

WASHING DISHES IN THE WOODS

Try to eat every last bite of your meal so there are no leftovers. To do your dishes, heat up a small pot of water and make rinse water by pouring a tablespoon of bleach in a gallon of cold water. Then, pick a spot about 200 feet away from your campsite and any source of clean water. Dig a hole 6 to 8 inches deep. Scrape the dishes into the hole, then scrub them with the hot water and biodegradable soap. Rinse them with the bleach solution.

Bury the dirty water and food scraps in the hole when you're finished. Afterward, store all the dishes, pots, and utensils you used, along with any scented items such as toothpaste and lotion, with all your food in the bear hang.

HANGING POT HOOK

There are two ways to make this handy adjustable hanger, both of which use the pot hook notch (see page 47). The easier method is to find a stick about an inch thick and at least a couple of feet long with a good bend at one end. The other method is to use a straight stick, which works just fine but requires cutting more notches.

WHAT YOU NEED

- A hardwood stick, about 1 inch thick,
  preferably with a 45-degree bend at one end
- A knife

BENT STICK	STRAIGHT STICK

Carve two or three pot hook notches on the opposite side of the stick from the bend at the top. Be sure to space the notches so that the end of the stick won't go into the pot if you hang it from the top notch.	Carve two or three pot hook notches in one end of the stick, then carve two or three more at the other end, but facing the opposite direction. Hang the stick over your fire from one end, then hang your pot from the other end.

bent stick
pot hook

THE ART OF SHELTER

There is something magical about creating a home in the woods, and staying overnight in a shelter you have built is an amazing rite of passage. Think of it as your reward for practicing so many survival skills! Getting enough sleep is one of the most important things you can do in a survival situation so that your body can rest and your mind can stay strong.

The great thing is, you don't need a tent to get a good night's sleep. You can make shelters in many different shapes and sizes, using both synthetic and natural materials. A simple tent made with a poncho or small tarp is great for warm summer nights, or you can build a snug debris hut that will help you stay warm in cooler weather.

A-FRAME TARP SHELTER

A waterproof layer offers the most versatile type of shelter. It can be set up in many different configurations to provide protection from the sun, wind, or rain. Here is one option for using a tree and some logs and rocks as supports; see page 106 for some other ideas.

WHAT YOU NEED

- 10 × 10-foot tarp, poncho, or emergency blanket (larger is fine)
- A straight pole, at least 6 feet long and about 2 inches thick
- 6 large rocks, heavy logs, or branches (tent stakes work, too)

- Pieces of paracord: one at least 15 feet long, one or two 8–10 feet long, and four 3–4 feet long (other lengths will work depending on your materials)
- Armfuls of small evergreen branches, pine needles, leaves, or other bedding material (optional)

1. Find a flat spot near a sturdy tree or branch. The tree will serve as your first anchor point. Fold your tarp in half and lay it on the ground so you know where your second anchor point (the straight pole) will go. Pick up your tarp and clear away all the rocks and sticks between the anchor points — anything that you don't want poking you in the back while you sleep! If you're using bedding material, lay it down where the tarp was.

2. Wrap one end of the longest piece of paracord around the tree, attaching it with a friction wrap knot (see page 74). This cord will become the ridgeline, or peak, of your tent. It should be at least hip high, depending on the size of your tarp. You want to be able to sit up in your shelter. If you have a larger tarp, you can tie the ridgeline higher to make a shelter you can stand up in.

   Pull the line out to your second anchor point, hold the straight pole straight up, and wrap the cord around the branch a couple of times at the same height as the knot on the tree. Make sure that you have a few feet of cord extending beyond the second anchor. Pull it really tight.

3. Wrap the extra length from the ridgeline several times around a rock or heavy log (or use tent stakes) and tie it off with a couple of half hitches. Place the rock at a distance from the pole so the cord is taut.

4. Tie an 8- to 10-foot piece of cord to the pole just above or below the first piece, using a friction wrap knot. Tie the other end to a second rock, and move the rock to pull the cord taut. Adjust both rocks as needed so the pole stands straight up and is evenly balanced between both stake lines. Make sure the ridgeline is taut enough to support your tarp. If necessary, add a third stake line.

You'll need to apply lots of tension as you set up your stakes so the ridgeline will support your tarp. Move back and forth between the support pole and the staking rocks to get the line good and tight. You can do this by yourself, but it does make it easier to have a friend helping.

5. Drape your tarp over the ridgeline and adjust it until it's hanging evenly.

6. Use the 3- to 4-foot pieces of paracord to stake out the corners of the tarp. Tie one end of a cord through the grommet of the tarp using an overhand on a bight. Wrap the other end around a log or rock to secure it. You can use a taut-line hitch to make the line adjustable.

Another way to attach the cord to the tarp is to fold the cord in half and poke the bight through the grommet. Insert a short, thick stick into the loop and pull the line tight on the other side, then tie the two ends of the line to whatever you are using as a stake.

TARP SHELTER VARIATIONS

The A-frame setup is just one of many ways to make a tarp into a shelter. Here are a couple of other ideas. Hiking poles, if you have them with you, make good tent poles as well.

A-Frame with Closed End

This type is a good choice for cooler weather or when it might rain.

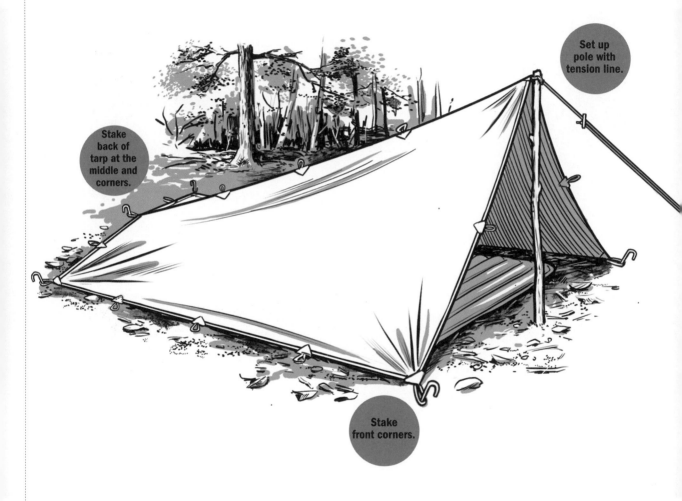

Set up pole with tension line.

Stake back of tarp at the middle and corners.

Stake front corners.

A-Frame with Open Sides

This type works when you want some shelter but the temperatures are warm.

Set up two poles with as many tension lines as needed to make a fly (extension) over your sleeping area.

Stake down four corners to make a floor.

DEBRIS HUT

Building a debris hut is like making a giant squirrel's nest! It's essentially an all-natural insulated sleeping bag and tent in one — and there's no need to cut down any live trees or other plants.

WHAT YOU NEED

- 1 ridgepole: a long forked pole, 3–4 inches thick and at least 1 foot longer than you are with your arms stretched overhead (If you can't find a forked branch, you can use a straight one. See the note in step 2.)

- 2 edge markers: long, straight branches about the same height as you are

- 1 support pole: a strong forked stick, 3–4 feet long

- 40–50 ribs: straight branches, 1–2 inches thick and 3–4 feet long

- 40–50 lattice branches: thin branches or twigs, less than ½ inch thick and 1–2 feet long

- Armloads of duff: leaves, pine needles, ferns, or other dry material from the forest floor

Debris huts work well in dense hardwood and pine forests where there are a lot of dead branches and a thick layer of organic material.

An east-facing opening lets in morning light and warmth.

1. Select a spot where you have plenty of materials to build with. Choose an anchor tree on high, well-drained ground, not in a hollow or near a floodplain. Before you begin to build, check for widow-maker branches hanging overhead (see page 86). Make sure you aren't building near poison ivy or a wasp's nest!

2. Orient the opening of your shelter to the east or south to take advantage of early sunlight for warmth and to help dry out your space during the day. The ridgepole is the backbone of your shelter. Wedge the fork against the anchor tree at about hip height. (**Note:** If you're using a straight ridgepole, prop it on a low branch or in a crotch of the anchor tree.)

Test your ridgepole by leaning on it before you begin to build. It has to be strong enough to hold up many pounds of debris.

3. Lie on your side under the ridgepole and measure with your elbow, as shown, to be sure you have enough headroom. Adjust the height of the ridgepole as needed. The tighter the space, the easier it is for your body heat to warm it up.

DEBRIS HUT continued

The space inside the hut needs to be snug so that it warms up quickly and holds that warmth all night.

support pole

4. Place the edge markers on either side of the ridgepole, then lie on your back directly under the ridgepole. Adjust the edge markers so that each one is two hand-widths from your body and they are parallel to each other.

5. It's important to brace the ridgepole for extra support. Set the fork of the support pole under the ridgepole on the side where your entrance will be.

If the ribs extend too much over the ridgepole, they can create spots for water to get in.

6. Place one rib branch about 2 feet from the support pole to mark the entrance. Place the rest of the ribs along both sides of the ridgepole, 3 to 4 inches apart and leaning against it at about a 45-degree angle. You don't want the ends extending over the ridgepole more than a few inches, so break or cut the branches as needed.

Continue to place ribs along the back side of your shelter to make a solid wall. Don't fill in the whole front side, though. You need an entrance so you can get inside!

A strong lattice is critical for holding the debris layer.

7. Build a lattice by placing the smaller branches horizontally or at 45-degree angles across the ribs. This creates a structure that will hold up the debris and make your hut weatherproof and watertight.

Don't use ferns — they are full of moisture and will create dampness in your shelter.

8. Gather dry debris from around your anchor tree and drop it along the ridgepole so it covers both sides of the lattice. Keep piling it up until the entire structure is thickly covered. The colder the weather, the thicker the layer should be.

DEBRIS HUT continued

Elbow depth is fine for summer, but at other times of year, create a layer of debris as deep as your whole arm.

9. To be sure that your hut is waterproof, pour water over the ridgepole, then check to see if it stayed nice and dry inside. This is the true test of a good shelter!

10. Once you're sure the interior will stay dry in a rainstorm, line the interior of the hut with layers of debris. Make a thick layer on the ground and stuff debris along the edges and at the narrow end to close up all cracks.

11. Burrow yourself in so you have layers of debris surrounding your body and insulating you from the ground. On a really cold night, close off the entrance with your backpack for extra insulation and protection.

If you pack your hut properly, you actually have to burrow into it, like a squirrel. On really cold nights, pile extra debris outside the entrance so you can pull more in if you need it.

BATHROOM BASICS

A crucial part of a being a good camper is being prepared to dispose of your bathroom waste so that it doesn't pose a hazard to wildlife or to other people. It's important to keep your toilet area, sometimes called a "cathole," well away from your camp and any water source.

BATHROOM KIT

When camping overnight far away from a bathroom, always bring along the following items:

- Hand sanitizer gel or soap
- Toilet paper
- Trowel
  Pack each item in its own ziplock bag, then put all three bags in a larger one.

BATHROOM PROCEDURE

Depending on where you are camping, there may be specific rules about disposing of human waste. Some wilderness areas require you to pack out your poop, or at least your used toilet paper. Check the rules before you go!

To go to the bathroom in the wild, pick a spot about 200 feet from your camp and any water source. If you need to poop, dig a hole about 4 inches across and 6 inches deep. Girls can dig a smaller hole to pee in. Squat over the hole to go and dispose of your toilet paper in the hole. Use as little toilet paper as possible. Cover it all back up with dirt after you have finished. It's helpful to mark that spot with an X made of sticks or rocks, so you and your campmates know not to dig up that spot again!

If you're camping in one area for a few days, you might choose to dig a latrine trench, which is like a cathole that is several feet long. As people use it, they fill it in with a few handfuls of dirt to keep the smell down and flies away. Set up a signal so people know when the area is free — for example, hang a bandana when the latrine is in use. When you leave, cover the latrine well. If you return to that campsite, dig your next latrine in a different spot.

Be aware of gravity when you squat and make sure your feet are uphill from where your pee will land.

Don't be afraid to use a nearby tree for assistance!

A latrine trench works for a group of campers staying in one place for a few days.

TIP FROM THE GUIDE
THE BUDDY SYSTEM

Here's a good way to make a cathole that's a good distance from camp without getting lost on your way back. Find a buddy and together, walk until the camp is far away but still visible. Have your buddy wait there while you walk to a point where you have some privacy but can still see your buddy. Then you can swap spots. The other benefit is that your buddy can hold the hand sanitizer for you!

4

CAMP CRAFT

You've learned quite a few skills so far, enough to set up your campsite, make a shelter, and build a fire. Here's a chance to put those skills to work using natural resources from the forest to build all sorts of things for camp life, such as a walking stick, kitchen utensils, and extra rope. Have fun with these simple projects. The more you practice, the more elaborate you can make your items.

FROM STICK TO STAFF

Explorers throughout history have used walking staffs on their travels. A sturdy staff helps you set your pace and keep your balance on steep trails or while crossing a river. Use it as a ruler, a carrying pole for hauling water, or to support a tarp shelter. A good walking staff is a valuable wilderness companion!

Usually you should harvest only dead wood for projects, but your staff needs to be strong and flexible, so you need a long, straight piece of green wood. A staff that snaps in half when you put weight on it is no good! This project gives you a chance to practice the forward grip and the batoning technique.

WHAT YOU NEED

- A straight, green sapling or branch, ¾–1½ inches thick and a couple of feet taller than you are
- A knife

WHAT YOU DO

1. Cut your stick. Bend the sapling or branch toward the ground until the fibers are stretched to their limit. Hold your knife in a forward grip and place the blade facing straight down at the bend. Check for safe follow-through, then press down hard, rocking the knife back and forth in a seesaw motion to cut into the wood.

2. Cut off the small branches. Lay the stick on a log, wooden board, or other surface that won't damage the blade of your knife. Use the batoning technique (see page 50) to slice off all the smaller branches and twigs as close to the joint as possible.

Your staff should be taller than you are so the top point can't accidently injure your eyes. A longer stick also helps you set a good pace as you walk.

← Cut here

3. **Measure your staff.** Hold the branch next to you with the thicker end on the ground. Raise your arm and hold the other end with your extended hand. Mark a spot between your elbow and wrist to gauge the correct length. Use the rose petal cut (see page 45) to trim the top of the branch. Repeat on the other end to round off the bottom of the staff. This makes it less likely that the wood will split as it dries.

4. **Debark the stick.** Taking the bark off allows the staff to dry out over time and become lighter and stronger. It also prevents insects from burrowing under the bark, weakening the wood. Holding your knife in a forward grip, place the blade on your stick at just enough of an angle so you can cut off strips of bark without digging into the wood. Move the knife away from you in a slicing motion, keeping the blade just under the bark. Continue until you have peeled off all the bark.

WILDERNESS WISDOM
HARVEST LIKE A CARETAKER OF THE LAND

Be mindful that every shrub or sapling is a living thing. Look for where the tree stand is dense or there are two trees or branches rubbing against each other. This rubbing creates an opening in the bark, which makes the plant more vulnerable to disease. If you can, harvest these trees or branches rather than cutting down healthy ones.

SUN COMPASS

Here's a fun and simple way to use the sun to tell what direction is north. For best results, start making your sun compass before noon, when the sun is still at an angle, not directly overhead.

1. Cut a stick about 3 feet long and sharpen one end of it. Drive the stick into the ground in a flat, sunny spot.

2. Locate the very tip of the shadow and mark it with a stick or small rock.

TIP FROM THE GUIDE
THE SUN

The sun moves east to west, but shadows are like reflections in the mirror. Each new shadow marker, therefore, will be to the *east* of the previous marker. Depending on the contrast of the shadow, the time of day, the ground texture, or the shape of your stick, deciding precisely where the shadow stops may be tricky. You can lay something on the ground to help you see the shadow better: a light-colored shirt, a piece of birch bark or paper, even your hand.

3. Repeat step 2 every 15 minutes, three more times. You should now have four points marked on the ground. Make a line through the four points. This is your east–west line.

4. Lay another straight stick at a right angle to your east–west line, pointing away from the shadow-making stick. This line points straight north (if you are in the Northern Hemisphere).

FEATHER STICK

A feather stick is an important tool for lighting fires in wet conditions. It is also a fun way to practice your carving skills.

WHAT YOU NEED

- A branch of very dry hardwood (oak, ash, beech, or similar), 3–4 inches thick and at least 1 foot long
- A knife

WHAT YOU DO

1. With your knife, peel off any bark (the stick should be dry enough that most of the bark has already fallen off). Use the batoning technique (see page 50) to split the branch into sticks about 1 inch thick.

2. Hold a stick in one hand. Starting below your holding hand, carefully shave down thin strips of the inner wood without removing them, as shown in the photo at left. Make as many as you can in one spot, then move up a couple of inches and start again. Make three or four layers like this. Imagine that the flame has to climb a ladder, moving from layer to layer.

3. To use your feather stick to start a fire, hold it at an angle as shown in the photo below and ignite the feathered part. Let the flames catch and begin to burn the stick, then use it to start a pile of kindling.

At first, it's hard to get the right knife angle for making feathers. When you are first learning, practice shaving strips off the stick to use as tinder.

WOODEN SPOON

Carving a wooden spoon is a fun project that tests both your carving and your fire-making skills. You can make a larger spoon for stirring and serving food and a smaller one for eating.

WHAT YOU NEED

- A piece of wood (seasoned pine, basswood, or birch work well)
- A knife
- A pencil or piece of charcoal
- Embers from your firepit
- A round stone about the size you want the bowl of your spoon to be

WHAT YOU DO

1. Use the batoning technique (see page 50) to create a blank (the flat form that will become your spoon). The blank shown here is 1 foot long × 2 inches wide × 1 inch thick.

2. Carve a notch into each side of the blank, about a third of the way from one end.

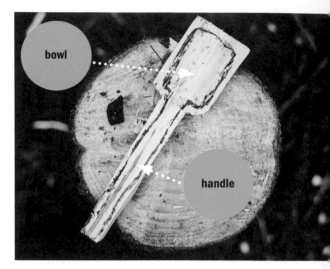

3. Using the notches as stop cuts, carve down the longer sides of the blank. This will be the handle.

4. Draw a spoon shape on the blank with a pencil or piece of charcoal from your fire.

If you do create a flame, blow sharply, like blowing out a candle, to extinguish it.

5. Carefully place an ember in the area you outlined for the bowl, using tongs (see page 128) or green sticks. Hold the ember in place and watch carefully so it doesn't burn too deeply. Blow gently on the ember but not hard enough to make it flame up. You want a shallow layer of char over the whole bowl area. You may need several embers. Make sure you return them all to the fire when you are done with them.

6. Let the charred area cool, then scrape out the burned parts with the stone until you uncover a fresh layer of wood.

7. Repeat steps 5 and 6 until the bowl of your spoon is as deep as you want it to be.

8. Use your knife to round off and smooth the bowl of the spoon. Carve the handle until it is smooth and comfortable to hold in your hand. Use a rose petal cut (see page 45) to round off the end.

TONGS

Tongs are very handy to have around your campfire. You can use them to pick up embers for igniting tinder, making a spoon (see page 125), shifting logs in your fire, or moving hot food.

WHAT YOU NEED

- 1 stick, about 1 inch thick and 18–24 inches long
- 1 stick or piece of scrap wood, about ½ thick and 2–3 inches long
- A knife
- 2 lengths of paracord or cordage, each 12–18 inches long

WHAT YOU DO

1. Use the batoning technique (see page 50) to carefully split the longer stick into two roughly even pieces. Match the flat sides of the stick back together. The thicker end will be your handle. Make a 4-inch loop near the end of one of the pieces of cord. Hold the curve of the loop at the handle end of the sticks, with the standing (short) end pointing toward the tips of the tongs. Wrap the working end of the cord around the sticks a couple of times to hold the loop in place.

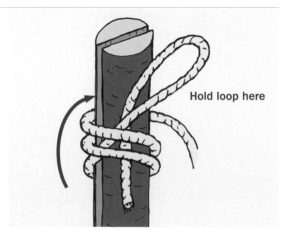

Hold loop here

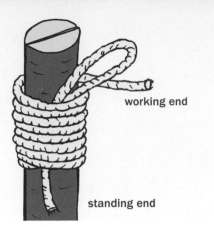

working end

standing end

2. Continue wrapping the cord tightly around the sticks, making sure the coils are close together. Leave the standing end sticking out. This is called "whipping."

3. Insert the working end of the wrapped cord through the loop.

4. Pull down on the standing end of the cord to bring the working end into the wraps and tighten the whip.

5. Wedge the small stick between the longer ones below the whip. Experiment with the placement until you can comfortably pinch the free ends of the sticks together to pick up an object. Lash the crosspiece in place with another piece of paracord, wrapping above and below it and tying it off with a simple overhand knot.

Wrap the cord above and below the crosspiece to keep it in place.

MAKING CORDAGE

It's good to know how to make cordage (string or rope) out of natural materials. What if you use all your paracord setting up camp and then need a few more pieces to make stake lines or hang up your gear? This project shows you how to make cordage from thin tree branches, but you can also use long grasses or other fibrous plants.

WHAT YOU NEED

- A bunch of fresh branches, at least ½ inch thick and 3–4 feet long
- A knife

WHAT YOU DO

1. Cut the thicker end of each branch at an angle, as shown.

2. Start peeling the bark from the pointed end of the branch. You want a couple of layers of the inner bark to come up as well.

3. Peel the first strip down a few inches, then start another strip.

4. Keep peeling until the end of the branch is bare and all the strips are about the same length.

5. Grab a handful of strips and slowly pull them off the branch. Make the strips at least 2 feet long, or longer if possible. Repeat until you have a pile of strips. The more strips you have, the longer your cordage will be.

6. To separate the strong inner bark that you'll use to make the cordage, pinch a strip to break the outer bark. Work the pinched part back and forth to make a tab you can grab onto.

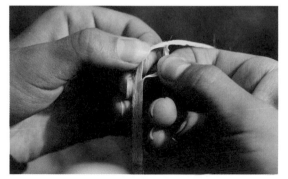

7. Holding the tab, carefully peel the bark away from the inner fibers.

8. Once you've removed all the bark, pull apart the strips of inner fiber into thinner strips.

MAKING C⊙RDAGE continued

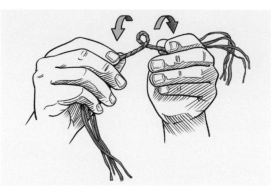

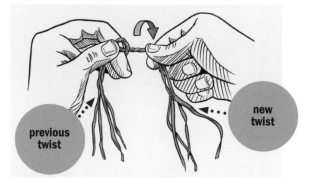

9. Gather three to six strips of similar length. Holding them in the middle, twist tightly in opposite directions, moving your fingers toward the ends of the strips. As the strips bind together and become tighter, the middle section will turn on itself to create a small loop. (I call this "the magic cross"!)

10. Pinch the loop between the thumb and index finger of one hand, with the two sections of fibers pointing down. Now you have one section of twisted fibers crossing in front of the other. Hold the front section with the ring and pinkie fingers of the same hand holding the loop. With your other index finger and thumb, take the fibers of the back strand and twist them away from you a few times to create a longer strand.

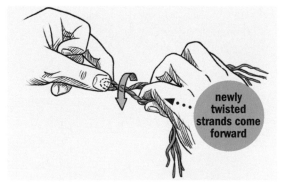

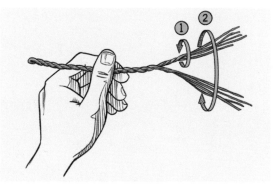

11. Still holding the loop, cross the newly twisted strand over the other strand to bring it in front, as shown above. Hold that strand with the ring and pinkie fingers of the same hand holding the loop, as in step 10, and with your opposite hand, pick up and twist a section of untwisted fiber (now in back) away from you.

12. Continue twisting short sections and crossing them over each other. After a few inches, you won't need to hold on to the original loop and can work your way along the remaining fibers until you get to the end. You can either tie off your cordage with a simple overhand knot or splice in more fibers to make it longer (see next page).

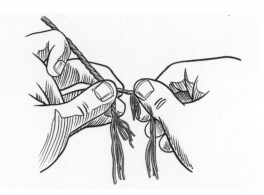

13. To splice in more fiber and make a longer piece of cordage, leave a few inches of untwisted fiber at the end of your first piece of cordage. Take another five or six strips and twist them in the middle as you did in step 9, but this time, instead of making a closed loop, just bend the twisted part in half to make a V. Line the V up with the ends of the existing cordage.

14. Holding the finished cordage and one half of the untwisted fibers in one hand, twist one of the short ends of the finished cordage with the other half of the new fibers. Twist away from you as in step 10 and then cross back over as in step 11. The short ends should now be twisted in with the new longer fibers.

15. Repeat with the other short end and the other half of the new fibers. Now you can continue as before to make as long a piece as you need!

TIP FROM THE GUIDE
PICKING YOUR PLANT MATERIAL

Different plants are easier or harder to work with depending on the season. Using branches, as shown here, is best during late spring and summer, when the trees are full of sap and the bark is easy to peel. Long grasses and sedges work better after you let them dry out for a while. Cattails and rushes can be used any time of year.

CAMOUFLAGE

Knowing how to camouflage yourself comes in handy when you want to see wild animals close-up in their natural habitat. When you do it correctly, you can be (almost) invisible! The key is preventing your skin (especially on your face) from reflecting light.

When you're done, see how well you can hide!

The order here is "Dull, dapple, fuzz."

1. Dull: Rub a light coating of mud all over your face, neck, and hair. Wet mud looks shiny at first, but as it dries, it becomes dull.

2. Dapple: Grind some charcoal into powder and mix it with a little water. Smear it across the high surfaces of your face (forehead, cheekbones, and the bridge of your nose) to create a dappled effect with no hard lines. Don't put it in hollow places, like around your eyes, as that makes them stand out more.

3. Fuzz: Crush a handful of dry leaves and pine needles and rub them on your skin, letting some stick to create texture.

5

FOOD & DRINK

Now that you've built your camp and have a fire going, it's time to do some cooking! Being out in the wilderness and setting up camp takes a lot of energy, and it's important to eat nutritious food and stay hydrated. In this chapter you'll learn some basic recipes and also how to find and purify water.

THE IMPORTANCE OF WATER

Humans can't survive very long without water. In fact, we can only live for three minutes without air, three days without water, and three weeks without food. You can see how important it is to have plenty of clean water on hand. You lose water as you sweat, pee, and even breathe, so always drink a lot of it when you are out in the woods being active.

TIP FROM THE GUIDE
LOOK TO THE TREES

Some species of trees can show you where there is water. Cottonwoods, willows, and basswoods all need lots of water to thrive. If you can identify them, you'll know water is nearby when you see them.

cotton-wood

willow

bass-wood

Going without water can make you very sick. Your hydration level affects your ability to think, make decisions, and perform physical tasks. When you are just 1 percent dehydrated, you lose 50 percent of your gripping strength. In addition, without enough water, you can't properly digest your food. So knowing how to find, collect, and purify water that you can drink and cook with is an essential survival skill.

DON'T DRINK THAT!

Before you learn how to harvest water, it's important to understand that most water in the wilderness isn't safe to drink. Even if a stream or pond looks clear and clean, it might be contain parasites that can cause diarrhea, vomiting, respiratory problems, and other illnesses. Both animals and humans can pollute water, so be aware of what sources of contamination might be around you. Don't collect water downstream from a beaver dam or a dairy farm or other agricultural site.

When you're looking for and collecting water, be cautious but don't worry too much! Even if you can't be certain that the water you find in the wilderness is safe to drink, there are many ways you can purify it. See page 143 for more about water purification.

GO TO THE SOURCE

Always try to collect from water that's moving, like streams and rivers. Stagnant water, like in a swamp, is dirtier. When you find a flowing stream, follow it uphill as far as possible and see if you can find the source, or spring, where the stream first comes out of the ground. You can dig a hole to create a well. When the sediment clears, you can collect the water.

See page 143 for more about water purification.

WILDERNESS WISDOM

LAW OF

According to the Law of 3s, a person can live:

3 minutes without air

3 days without water

3 weeks without food

3 hours without shelter (in a harsh environment)

The power of the mind, however, can alter these limitations (for better or for worse).

TIP FROM THE GUIDE
NEED A DRINK?

Check whether you're dehydrated using this test.

1. While you're standing up, take your pulse for a full minute. Write down the number. This is your baseline pulse.

2. Lie down, wait 1 minute, then take your pulse again for a full minute. Write down the number.

3. Subtract your lying-down pulse rate from your standing-up pulse rate. If the difference is more than 10, you're dehydrated.

   For example. . .

   97 (standing-up pulse) –
   86 (lying-down pulse) = **11**
   Drink more water!

HARVESTING WATER

There are lots ways to collect water when you aren't near a stream. Here are some of them.

COLLECT DEW

At night, as the air cools but the ground remains warm, condensation forms on grass and other plants. In the morning, you can harvest the dew by soaking it up with your bandana, being careful to avoid collecting dirt from the ground. When your bandana is soaking wet, squeeze it into a container. You can also collect the dew that forms on the outside of your tent or tarp.

Another method that works overnight is to place a plastic bag over the end of a leafy plant. Seal the bag with cordage or paracord. The condensation will pool in the bag.

Another method is to set up a tarp as a funnel to channel dew or rainwater into a container.

CAPTURE RAINWATER

When it rains, look around for the places where water naturally collects, like indentations in rocks, trees, and hard-packed ground. Collect some big oval leaves to scoop the rainwater into a container.

GO GREEN

Some plants have water inside them that you can drink in a pinch. Here are a couple of examples.

Grapevine. Wild grapevines grow up over trees. Find where the vine comes up and cut the stem at an angle 2 or 3 feet from the ground. Bend the stem over a container and tie it into place to drain.

Thistle. Be careful when handling a thistle and wear gloves if you have any. The prickers on a thistle can be very tiny and hard to see, so make sure you use your knife to thoroughly scrape them off the stem of the plant! Chew on the celery-like stalk to extract the water, then spit out the fibers.

BUILD A SOLAR STILL

A solar still works by using the sun to evaporate moisture from the earth. When the moisture hits the plastic sheet, it condenses and drips into the collection vessel. A solar still needs to be located in an area that will receive sun for as much of the day as possible.

WHAT YOU NEED

- A shovel
- A container for collecting water
- A sheet of clear plastic, about 4 × 4 feet
- Small rock or other weight
- A few large rocks

WHAT YOU DO

1. Dig a hole about 1½ feet across and about 2 feet deep.

2. Put the container at the bottom of the hole.

3. Cover the opening of the hole with the plastic, holding it in place with a few large rocks. Place the small rock or weight in the middle of the plastic and gently push it down to create a depression over the container.

4. Finish sealing the outside edges of the plastic sheet with more rocks, or with dirt or sand dug from the hole.

5. After a few hours (depending on the temperature and humidity), condensation will begin to form and drip into the container. When you roll back the plastic, be careful not to get dirt in the container.

You can use a length of plastic tubing to siphon water out of the container, but it isn't necessary.

weight positioned over container

clear plastic

condensation

collection container

PURIFYING WATER

There are several ways you can make sure your water is clean and safe enough to drink. Here are some of them.

BOIL IT

Boiling water kills bacteria, viruses, protozoa, and parasites. Make sure the water comes to an active boil — with dancing bubbles, not just little ones on the inside of the pot — so you can be certain that all the pathogens are killed. Let it boil longer at higher elevations (because water boils at a lower temperature above 5,000 feet). **Note:** Boiling does *not* remove chemicals or toxins from the water.

FILTER IT

Many filters are small and handheld, making them easy to take camping with you. Some are operated by pumping a handle, others are bags that hang and work with gravity, and there are even filters that fit right in your water bottle. Sawyer and RapidPure brand filters are compact, field-ready, and easy to clean.

ADD IODINE

Iodine is a naturally occurring element and an essential nutrient. It also is an effective natural disinfectant that kills many, but not all, of the most common pathogens present in natural fresh water sources. Follow the directions for adding iodine tablets to water. **Note:** Some people are allergic to iodine.

ADD BLEACH

You can add chlorine bleach to water to make it potable but do so very carefully. According to the Centers for Disease Control and Prevention, you should first filter the water (you can use your bandana). Add just two drops of plain, unscented bleach per quart of water (eight drops per gallon), stir well, and let it stand for at least half an hour. There should still be a slight odor of chlorine.

STIR IN SOME UV

The battery-powered Steripen uses ultraviolet light rays to sterilize clear water. Read and follow the directions carefully!

CAMPFIRE COOKING AND BAKING

From the simple snacks shown here to hot, nutritious dinners, all food tastes great when you've been outside all day!

STEAMED CORN ON COALS

Soak ears of corn, with the husks still on, in water for about 5 minutes. Place on a bed of embers for several minutes, turning a few times to prevent burning. Carefully peel back the husk; when the kernels are bright yellow and you can smell the corn, the corn is fully cooked.

BANANA BOAT

Make two cuts down a banana peel to create a flap. Pull back the
flap, then cut a wedge down the length of the banana and remove it.
Fill the space with mini marshmallows, chocolate chips, and graham
cracker bits or cereal. Cover with the flap and place the banana in a
bed of embers until the marshmallows and chocolate melt.

BANNOCK

This easy camp bread was staple fare for French-Canadian voyageur fur traders who roamed many miles during a whole season of trapping. There are lots of variations, since people have traditionally made it using whatever ingredients were available locally. You can easily make your own version over your campfire for a quick energy boost. For each piece of bannock, prepare a peeled stick, about 1 inch thick and 3 feet long. Round off the end with a rose petal cut (see page 45).

WHAT YOU NEED

- 2 cups all-purpose flour
- 2 teaspoons baking powder

Water
Optional additions: salt, brown sugar, dried fruit, nuts

WHAT YOU DO

1. Mix the flour and baking powder in a dish. Gently work enough water into the flour until the mixture is about the consistency of pizza dough. Mix in any additional ingredients. Break the dough into three or four pieces, each about the size of a fist.

2. Knead each piece by folding it over on itself a few times, using both hands. Roll the pieces into logs about 1 inch thick and a few inches long.

3. Wrap the dough around the end of the stick, spiraling it downward from the tip. Cover the tip of the stick with dough so the wood doesn't char.

Your fire needs to have a good bed of embers to give a steady, even heat. Flames will burn the outside of the bread without cooking the inside.

4. Hold the stick over the fire, rotating it so the dough cooks evenly without burning. Pay attention to the bottom part where the dough is thicker. The cooking time will depend on how hot your fire is. Test for doneness by tapping on the surface to see if there's a good crust.

CANDIED APPLE

Pierce an apple with a
sharpened stick (if desired, you
can peel the apple first). Heat
the apple over a low flame or
slow-burning embers, rotating
it often to prevent burning.
Coat the warm apple with brown
sugar, then rotate it over the
embers until the sugar melts.

S'MORES

Everyone loves this classic treat! Roast your marshmallow to the desired gooeyness. Place a piece of chocolate on a graham cracker and use a second graham cracker to take the marshmallow off the stick and close up the sandwich.

KEEP ON EXPLORING!

Once you've started on the path to not just surviving but thriving in the wilderness, you'll want to learn more about all aspects of life outdoors. The great thing is, you never stop learning — every time you go for a hike or spend a few nights camping out, you have the chance to hone your skills and discover new things.

On the next few pages, you'll find a little more information about wilderness skills, as well as my recommendations for books and websites that will expand your base of knowledge.

LEARN MORE
Books

Canterbury, Dave. *Bushcraft 101: A Field Guide to the Art of Wilderness Survival*. Adams Media, 2014.

Gilpatrick, Gil. *Outdoor Adventure Trips: Expert Advice on Camping, Canoeing, Hunting, Fishing, Hiking & Other Adventures in the Woods*. Heliconia Press, 2013.

Kochanski, Mors. *Basic Safe Travel and Boreal Survival Handbook: Gems from Wilderness Arts and Recreation Magazine*. Karamat Wilderness Ways, 2015.

——. *Bushcraft: Outdoor Skills and Wilderness Survival*. Lone Pine, 2016.

Mears, Raymond. *Essential Bushcraft: A Handbook of Survival Skills from around the World*. Hodder & Stoughton Ltd., 2003.

Zawalsky, Bruce. *Canadian Wilderness Survival*. Liard Books, 2017.

Websites and Programs

8 Shields
www.8shields.org

Creek Stewart
www.creekstewart.com

Children and Nature Network
www.childrenandnature.org

Flying Deer Nature Center
www.flyingdeernaturecenter.org

Hawk Circle Wilderness Education
www.hawkcircle.com

Karamat Wilderness Ways
www.karamat.com

Maine Primitive Skills School
www.primitiveskills.com

National Parks Every Kid Outdoors Campaign
www.nationalparks.org/our-work/campaigns-initiatives/every-kid-outdoors

NOLS (National Outdoor Leadership School)
www.nols.edu

Nature Watch Blog
www.nature-watch.com/blog/

Outdoor Living Wilderness School
www.owlschool.org

Outward Bound
www.outwardbound.org

The Tracker School
www.trackerschool.com

Wilderness Awareness School
www.wildernessawareness.org

TIP FROM THE GUIDE
CHECK OUT MY VIDEOS!

As with a well-balanced backpack, there's only so much stuff you can put in one book! For more detailed information on many of the projects introduced in this book, and some cool other ones like learning to make a bow drill to start a fire, visit www.earthworkprograms.com/book. I've posted some instructional videos there along with more material on learning to feel at home in the wilderness.

WEATHER FORECASTING

You should always check the forecast when planning an outdoor adventure, but instead of relying on a weather app to alert you to possible changes, learn to keep an eye on the sky. Weather conditions can shift rapidly, with rain or snow blowing in more quickly than you thought or a big thunderstorm suddenly forming overhead.

Identifying different kinds of clouds can help you know what to expect from the weather. Watching them can tell you what direction the wind is blowing and if the weather is changing. There are a few basic types of clouds, each with variations that depend on temperature, the amount of moisture in the air, and other factors.

LEARN MORE

Books

Ludlum, David M. *National Audubon Society Field Guide to North American Weather.* Alfred A. Knopf, 1991.

Rupp, Rebecca. *Weather!* Storey Publishing, 2003.

Sloane, Eric. *Eric Sloane's Weather Book.* BN Publishing, 2012.

Websites

For Spacious Skies
www.forspaciousskies.net

National Weather Service: Just for Kids
www.weather.gov/cae/justforkids.html

Cirrus clouds are the thin, wispy white clouds that spread out high in the sky. A few indicate pleasant weather, but if you see more gathering, a change may be coming.

Stratus clouds create an overcast day by covering most of the sky. They can be gray or white and often bring rain or snow.

Cumulous clouds are low, puffy, white clouds that look solid and may appear to take on shapes. They usually indicate fair weather.

Cumulonimbus clouds are huge, tall clouds with dark bases that usually accompany heavy rain, as well as thunder and lightning.

FORAGING EDIBLE PLANTS

Nature is full of food if you know where to look. Many plants are not only safe to eat but also delicious *and* nutritious. Learning which plants are edible at what times of year is a valuable skill.

The cattail, or bull rush, is just one example of a common plant that might surprise you with its many uses, both edible and otherwise. My mentor, Tom Brown, called it "the supermarket of the swamp" because it can provide you with so much.

You can eat the tender shoots and stems in salads, soups, and stir-fries. The brown seed heads (the actual "cattail") can be roasted when young. The nutritious pollen that appears in midsummer can be collected and added to pancakes or soups and stews. The root can be dried and pounded into flour.

In addition to its value as a food, you can use the narrow leaves of cattails to make cordage (see page 130) and rope. Mature cattails can be dipped in oil or fat and lit as torches. And the fluffy seeds make excellent tinder and can add a layer of insulation for warmth.

LEARN MORE

Books

Haines, Arthur. *Ancestral Plants: A Primitive Skills Guide to Important Wild Edible, Medicinal, and Useful Plants of the Northeast.* Volumes 1 and 2, Anaskimin, 2010, 2015.

Peterson, Lee Allen. *Peterson Field Guide to Edible Wild Plants: Eastern/Central North America.* Houghton Mifflin Company, 1977.

Thayer, Samuel. *The Forager's Harvest: A Guide to Identifying, Harvesting, and Preparing Edible Wild Plants.* Foragers Harvest Press, 2006.

———. *Nature's Garden: A Guide to Identifying, Harvesting, and Preparing Edible Wild Plants.* Foragers Harvest Press, 2010.

Zachos, Ellen. *Backyard Foraging.* Storey Publishing, 2013.

Websites

Forager's Harvest
www.foragersharvest.com

Wild Edible
www.wildedible.com

OBSERVING WILDLIFE

One of the most wonderful things about being out in the wilderness is learning about all the creatures that live there. You may not see many animals and birds at first, especially if you're walking fast or talking, but if you slow down and spend time quietly watching, you'll begin to realize that you're sharing your campsite or your hiking trail with many other beings.

Learning to spot signs of wildlife is like learning to read a special kind of book. Following a set of tracks, or spoor, can tell a story about a fox hunting a mouse or a turkey digging through leaves to find insects. A pile of poop, called scat, can tell you that a coyote or skunk was in the area.

Sounds can tell you a lot, too. Even if you can't see birds in leafy trees, knowing their calls can tell you what kind of bird they are and even what they're saying. Many birds give alarm calls, which can alert you to an intruding hawk or other threat.

LEARN MORE
Books

Elbroch, Mark, and Kurt Rinehart. *Peterson Reference Guide to Behavior of North American Mammals.* Houghton Mifflin Harcourt, 2011.

Young, Jon. *What the Robin Knows: How Birds Reveal the Secrets of the Natural World.* Houghton Mifflin Harcourt, 2012.

Websites

Cornell Lab of Ornithology
www.allaboutbirds.org
National Audubon Society
www.audubon.org
National Geographic Society
www.nationalgeographic.com
National Wildlife Federation
www.nwf.org

the hawk's dinner

raccoon tracks

HONING YOUR NAVIGATION SKILLS

At first your outdoor adventures may take place in the woods near your home or in a well-traveled wilderness area with marked trails. As you continue to learn and become a more experienced hiker and camper, you'll want to expand your horizons and get off the beaten path. Once you're away from those marked trails, it's critical to know how to orient yourself and to figure out what direction you want to go. The more you know, the less likely you are to get lost, and if you do get lost, the more likely you are to find your way again.

Learn as much as you can by practicing your map and compass skills. Check out orienteering programs, which set a course for people to follow within a certain time frame. Read about how the night sky and constellations can help you know where you are even when it's dark.

LEARN MORE
Books

Caudill, Craig, and Tracy Trimble. *Essential Wilderness Navigation: A Real-World Guide to Finding Your Way Safely in the Woods With or Without a Map, Compass or GPS*. Page Street Publishing, 2019.

Gooley, Tristan. *The Lost Art of Reading Nature's Signs: Use Outdoor Clues to Find Your Way, Predict the Weather, Locate Water, Track Animals — and Other Forgotten Skills*. The Experiment, 2015.

Singleton, Robert. *You'll Never Get Lost Again: Simple Navigation for Everyone*. Atlantic Publishing Group, 2018.

Websites
Orienteering USA
www.orienteeringusa.org

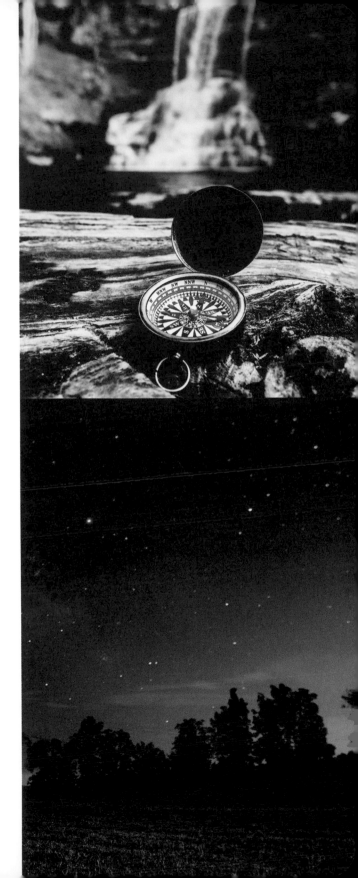

LEARNING FIRST AID

Accidents can happen even when you're prepared and being very careful. That's why you should always carry a first-aid kit with you, whether you're out for an afternoon hike or setting up camp for several days. It's also a good idea to take a basic first-aid course to learn how to stop bleeding, bandage minor wounds, and put on a simple splint. And while prevention is the best cure, it's also good to know how to deal with things like bug and tick bites, exposure to poisonous plants, and sunburn.

LEARN MORE

Books

ACEP First Aid Manual 5th Edition: The Step-by-Step Guide for Everyone. DK, 2014.

Mars, Brigitte. *The Natural First Aid Handbook: Household Remedies, Herbal Treatments, and Basic Emergency Preparedness Everyone Should Know*. Storey Publishing, 2017.

Websites

American Red Cross

www.redcross.org

TIP FROM THE GUIDE

DEALING WITH TICKS

Ticks are found in most parts of the United States and are especially common in the Northeast. Many ticks carry infections like Lyme disease, so it's very important to protect yourself against them. Ticks hang out on blades of grass or low plants, waiting for an animal to pass by. They attach themselves to animals and people and suck blood, then fall off. To deter them, you can spray insect repellent around your ankles and legs. You can also tuck your pant legs into your hiking boots and tuck in your shirt so they can't get under your clothes. Wearing bright-colored clothing helps make the ticks stand out more if they're crawling on you.

Check your whole body for ticks after hiking or camping. Ticks are very tiny and can be hard to spot. If you find a tick embedded in your skin, don't panic! Just get a pair of tweezers and grab onto the tick as close to your skin as you can get and pull steadily upward until the tick comes out. You can also buy special tick removal tools. Other methods you may have heard of, like burning or smothering the tick, don't work and can lead to infection.

Once the tick is out, put it in a container with some isopropyl alcohol. Wash the area thoroughly with soap and water. Check with your doctor about having the tick tested for any diseases.

INDEX

Page numbers in *italics* indicate photos or illustrations.

Additional photography by © apomares/iStock.com, 152 top; © BanksPhotos/iStock.com, 138 center; © Birute/iStock.com, 152 2nd from bottom; © blickwinkel/Alamy Stock Photo, 87 top; Bryan Minear/Unsplash, 155 top; © Byrdyak/iStock.com, 57 bottom; © dlerick/iStock.com, 138 left; © DIMUSE/iStock.com, 143; © endlessadventure/iStock.com, 154 right; © filmfoto/iStock.com, 138 right; © Floortje/iStock.com, 24 bottom; © GoodLifeStudio/iStock.com, 152 2nd from top; © Jordana Meilleur/Alamy Stock Photo, 87 bottom; © Kerrick/iStock.com, 156; © Maksim Shebeko/stock.adobe.com, 152 bottom; © marekuliasz/iStock.com, 57 top; © Panther Media GmbH/Alamy Stock Photo, 87 middle; Seth Fink/Unsplash, 155 bottom; © Song_about_summer/stock.adobe.com, 15; Vincent Guth/Unsplash, 150; Vincent Van Zalinge/Unsplash, 154 left

SOME QUICK METRIC CONVERSIONS

Distance

1 inch = 2.54 centimeters	
1 foot = 30.5 centimeters	
1 yard = 0.9 meter	
1 mile = 1.6 kilometers	

Volume

1 teaspoon = 5 milliliters	
1 tablespoon = 15 milliliters	
1 cup = 240 milliliters	
4 cups (1 quart) = 0.95 liter	
4 quarts (1 gallon) = 3.8 liter	

ACKNOWLEDGMENTS

It has been an incredible journey in wilderness skills, and I am indebted to many teachers, mentors, and friends.

Ricardo Sierra introduced me to wilderness camps and rites of passage for youth. Tim Smith graciously invited me to his school and introduced me to the legendary Mors Kochanski, who I learned so much from and who became an advisor for our school.

Jeff Gotlieb opened the door for me to teach nationally and connect with experts throughout the world.

Walt Gigandet mentored me in the most in-depth way I've experienced: At one point he had me carve a bow drill set and make a fire BLINDFOLDED! I felt like I was the star pupil of the TV series *Kung Fu*.

I have story after story of mentoring relationships that I cannot fit here but that live in my heart, along with other mentors and friends: Mark Elbroch, Michael Pewtherer, Barry Keegan, Arthur Haines, Charlie Paquin, Tom Brown, Jon Young, Sam Thayer, Grandfather Great Blue Heron, Grandma Delta, Darry Wood, Snowbear, Russell Cutts, Larry Montalto, Greg Kowalski, Lenore Anderson, Lorene Wapotich, Fred Bixby, Walker Korby, James McNaughton, Tom Elpel, Kevin Reeve, Sara Little Crow Russell, Michael Haynack, Michael Kohout, Sue Morse, Ben Feeley, Farlin Black, Blanch Derby, Pierre Blinn, David Sharpe, John Chilkotowski, Alan Emond, and so many more.

EXPLORE YOUR WORLD
with More Books from Storey

BY CLARE WALKER LESLIE

Discover dozens of interactive projects for every season, with fun prompts to record daily sunrise and sunset times, draw a local map, keep a moon journal, or collect leaves to identify.

BY MARK WILSON

Dramatic photos reveal the lives of 19 North American owl species as they nest, fly, and hunt. You'll learn about these birds' silent flight, remarkable eyes and ears, haunting calls, and fascinating behaviors.

BY DEVIN FRANKLIN

Become a nature adventurer! Fifteen exercises in tracking, mapping, and observation will sharpen your senses, teach you to read nature's clues, and help you discover the wild residents that share your favorite outdoor spaces.

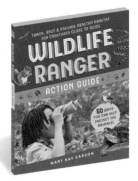

BY MARY KAY CARSON

Build a nesting box for birds and an abode for toads. With these habitat creation projects, you can make the world a better place for animals, starting right in your own backyard.